Making Miniature Country Houses

Sharon Pierce & Herb Surman

Sterling Publishing Co., Inc.   New York

DEDICATION

This book is lovingly dedicated
to the memory of Herb Surman,
our husband, father, "papa,"
and friend.

THANK YOU

To Gloria, Herb's wife, who took over building
the projects where Herb left off, and to whom
we can offer thanks for all the finishing touches
and the painting of each "little house."

To Randy, who willingly gave of his time to key
this manuscript into the word processor.

S.P.

Love and deep appreciation to Sharon Pierce,
whose dedication has brought the publication
of this book to fruition.

G.S.

Edited by Rodman Neumann

Library of Congress Cataloging-in-Publication Data

Pierce, Sharon.
    Making miniature country houses / by Sharon Pierce &
Herb Surman.
       p.   cm.
    ISBN 0-8069-6984-9
    1. Miniature craft.   2. Woodwork.   3. Architectural
models.
    I. Surman, Herb. II. Title.
    TT178.P54   1990
    728'.37'0228—dc20   89-48857
                                       CIP

Copyright © 1990 by Sharon Pierce and Herb Surman
Published by Sterling Publishing Co., Inc.
387 Park Avenue South, New York, N.Y. 10016
Distributed in Canada by Sterling Publishing
% Canadian Manda Group, P.O. Box 920, Station U
Toronto, Ontario, Canada M8Z 5P9
Distributed in Great Britain and Europe by Cassel PLC
Artillery House, Artillery Row, London SWIP IRT, England
Distributed in Australia by Capricorn Ltd.
P.O. Box 665, Lane Cove, NSW 2066
Manufactured in the United States of America
All rights reserved
Library of Congress Catalog Card No.: 89-48857
Sterling ISBN 0-8069-6984-9   Paper

CONTENTS

Color section follows page 64.

❖ Preface ❖

This book is filled with plans for making delightful little houses, churches, and an outstanding 1900s barn. I am happy to share with you the designs of a very special and talented man, Herb Surman.

Unfortunately for all of us, Herb passed away before he could complete all of the houses we had originally planned, which makes this book an even greater treasure for the many wonderful miniature buildings it does contain.

The houses in this book make outstanding display pieces that will give visual emphasis to any area of the home or office. And, if you are so inclined, they can be distinctive gifts that will likely become cherished heirlooms.

An option that can be exercised with virtually any of the projects is to leave the back open. The house with no back wall could then be used as a working dollhouse to furnish and add wonderful things, such as fireplaces with mantels, stairways, attics, etc.

These houses can be put to further use in their original calling as toy houses for play. A modern adaptation could be for use with model railroads or motorized miniature car tracks.

These miniature houses make a dramatic effect for any holiday, and especially at Christmastime with little lights placed inside and the houses set amid greenery and berries.

They can also be incorporated into a table centerpiece.

Another idea is to make your miniature house into a birdhouse! Simply trim the windows and doors without cutting them out, only cutting an entrance hole for the birds and maybe adding a perch. Then mount the base on a support pole.

You have many options available when you are constructing any of the projects in this book. And, although precise step-by-step instructions are provided, you will easily be able to add or delete items such as trim, porches, shutters, etc. to your own satisfaction, making each construction into your own design. Your choice of color alone can change any project dramatically.

Before you begin any of these projects, I urge that you take time to read over the chapters on General Instructions and on Materials and Equipment. These pages include basic information, hints, and tips that are applicable for every project as well as general principles that are not always stated for individual projects.

Although I sincerely wish that Herb had lived to share more of his talents with us, I know you will thoroughly delight in the making of these wonderful "little houses that Herb built"!

—Sharon Pierce

History of Early Buildings and ❖ Houses ❖

In the earliest of times, man lived in caves and trees, and anywhere he could find shelter. As man learned to make simple tools, he also learned to form small blocks from clay that could be dried in the sun.

Around 3100 B.C. the Egyptians were making flat-topped homes of sun-baked mudbrick. About 2600 years later the Assyrians among others started firing and glazing the bricks, making a harder, stronger brick.

All over the world, different types of houses were built reflecting the climate as well as the natural materials available and the dangers that were imminent. These structures were fashioned from grasses, wood, mud, clay bricks, and stone.

As time passed, man improved his shelter by incorporating fireplaces, windows that opened, elaborate stairways, porches, and eventually indoor plumbing.

Early European colonists to reach North America built log cabins of timber. After the settlements were started, however, many of the colonists built homes resembling the ones that they remembered from England or Holland. To make a warmer house, because of the more rigorous winters than they had experienced in England, the New Englanders built a great central chimney and plank floors, and they devised a blanket of overlapping clapboards, or sometimes shingles, to keep out the cold winds.

In the South, high ceilings helped keep rooms cooler in summer, and many porches were built to help shade the interior of the house.

Styles of houses and buildings have varied widely. Many designs can be traced to particular geographic regions and periods of time.

Colonial-style houses date back to the American colonial period of the 1600s and 1700s. Georgian and Victorian houses developed from styles that originated in Great Britain during the 1700s and 1800s.

The ranch house, which became one of the most popular styles in the United States during the mid-1900s, developed from early homes in the West and Southwest. The ranch-style houses are one level structures often with extensive porches.

Over the centuries, many of these styles have been built as miniature houses by a parent, an itinerant craftsman or, perhaps, the local cabinetmaker—primarily to serve the purposes of play, as toy buildings.

Little buildings are also constructed by architects to be used as models for structures that may eventually be built.

Whatever the style or styles of house you choose to build from this book, you can be sure that you are helping to preserve a little piece of history.

❖ Designing a Miniature House ❖

You don't have to figure out everything at once to begin designing the little house you want to build. But you may already have a general idea in mind. Certainly you will want to consider what styles appeal to you.

As you work through the choices that need to be made, you will find that the design takes shape and becomes clearer with each option you consider.

Once you have decided on the style of house you would like to make, the next thing is to determine the size. Should it be six inches tall, ten inches, twelve inches? Considering where the house might be displayed can help you decide the appropriate scale.

If you intend to make the house as a gift, think carefully about whether the person you will be presenting it to has ample space for the size you have in mind—better too small than too large.

Next you will want to decide how simple or complex the design of your house will be. Of course, if you are designing your first little house, a simple design would be the wisest choice to start with. Even if you have chosen a Victorian style, you can still make the design a simple one.

Make several different sketches to help you decide on porches, dormers, chimneys, shutters, etc. (You can look at general magazines, architectural or home-design magazines, and books for ideas.) Sketch your design with and without siding. You certainly don't need professional-looking sketches, just basic free-hand sketches will be fine. Also, you will probably want to sketch your house design with a few different roof angles.

While you are deciding on the main features, be sure to consider the number of windows and placement of the doors and windows.

Now you are ready to work out the exact dimensions of each wall, window, and door. You can also decide on the measurements of any chimneys, dormers, and the like at this time, or you may prefer to wait until the house is "under construction."

When choosing a color scheme, perhaps the very first consideration is whether you would like the house to look new or old, as achieving this look is dependent on the manner in which you paint it. For an old look choose muted color and possibly incorporate some "crackling" (page 11).

When selecting the color or multiple colors, first prepare a basic sketch. Then, using colored pencils, try a couple of different color combinations until you reach the most pleasing one.

Basically, remember that a series of choices needs to be made before you start construction. The following summary can serve as a reminder as you prepare your design and get ready to build.

Style and Size

Roof Style—Roof Angles

High peak
Flat
Slant

Surfaces

Stucco (paint mixed with sand)
Brick (paint to give effect)
Siding
  painted
  stained
Painted
Painted and aged (old crackled look)

Roofing Material

Tin
Wood
Shingles
Slate (painted wood roof or shingles)

Color

Single color
Multiple colors
  color combination

❖ General Instructions ❖

The first step in making any project is to gather the needed materials and to make sure that you have the proper equipment. Also, it is always a good idea to read through the entire directions before you start building the project. These general instructions present steps in construction shared by most, if not all, of the projects.

Once you are ready to begin construction, the next step is to transfer the measurements of the main pieces of the building onto a board of the correct thickness. It is important to use the same *actual measured thickness* as in the materials list, otherwise most of the other dimensions will have to be altered.

If you have access to a carpenter's square, or framing square, you will find that it is an excellent time-saver when you are drawing walls that must be square. When possible, to ensure the greatest strength for each piece and ultimately for your structure, draw patterns onto the wood so that the longer dimension of the pattern aligns with the lengthwise grain of the wood.

Once you've done the layout on the wood, you're ready to start by cutting out the larger pieces, such as the house walls and subroof. Then cut out window and door openings in those pieces. Now is the time to sand each piece. Also remember to sand all the other pieces as soon as they are cut (Illus. 1).

For most houses the rectangular-shaped walls, usually the front and back, butt against

the peaked walls (otherwise you will have to sand or plane the short wall to match the roof angle of the peaked wall). Spread a thin bead of glue on the inside face along the margins, or "side" edges, of the front and back sections. Glue these to the side sections, checking to make sure all of the corners are square. With a tack hammer, carefully tap in several brads along each corner.

A delightful option that you can keep in mind as you begin any project is to leave the back wall off for an "open" house. The open

Illus. 1. Sand each piece, by hand or machine, after it is cut to size.

house can be furnished, and a second floor with stairs can be added.

To add the floor, or base, set the house construction on a piece of ¼" wood, then pencil around the inside perimeter. Cut out the piece carefully just along the outside of the pencil line. Glue and then nail the floor to the house.

Cut a roof ridge to support the roof. This can be cut with the grain from a ¾" × ¾" strip to match the inside dimension between roof peaks. Glue and then nail the ridge between both peaks.

Make the window, door, and corner trim from ½" wood. You will need strips that are cut to ⅛" thickness. You can cut these with a radial-arm or table saw using a rip fence. You can also use a band saw with a guide, or for any of these saws you can make a simple guide by clamping a block of wood ⅛" from the blade (Illus. 2). Using the band saw will waste less wood since the blade is thinner.

After the strips are cut, then cut them to fit, first the horizontal window and door trim pieces. Glue these into place flat against the cutout edge, making the inward edge of the trim flush with the inside wall of the house.

Then cut the vertical pieces, attaching them in the same manner (Illus. 3).

Corner trim should be cut to match the height of the rectangular-shaped wall.

Siding can be considered optional whether called for or not. If it is not added when called

Illus. 3. *Gluing window trim in place.*

Illus. 2. *Cutting siding strips with the radial-arm saw.*

for, however, cut the window, door, and corner trim from ⅜"-wide wood so it will not protrude more than a slight amount.

To make siding, cut long strips ⅛" × ¾" from ¾" wood. Then cut the pieces to fit between the corner trim pieces for each wall. Work on one wall at a time, and start by gluing a piece flush with the bottom of the house. Attach each successive strip above the previous one with an even overlap of ⅛". Notch the strip to fit around window and door trim as needed (Illus. 4).

Illus. 4. Attaching siding.

You can choose to make the roof from various materials, such as tin, copper, ⅛" pine, pine or cedar shingles, using ⅛" luan plywood for a subroof.

If you choose to use tin or copper, simply use a pair of metal cutters to cut a piece of the metal approximately 1½" wider and 1½" longer than the total roof measurement. Then bend the metal in half, usually with the crease parallel to the long dimension.

Predrill holes, using a drill press, if available, where the roof will be nailed to the house. Tack in place using brads.

For a pine roof, cut from ⅛" pine two roof pieces that are slightly larger than the roof area obtained by measuring outside walls. Apply glue and nail the pieces in place. Then cut a ⅛" × ⅛" square strip to fit in the space between the pieces along the roofline, and glue this piece into place.

To make a shingled roof, first cut two pieces of ⅛" luan plywood to match the measurement of the roof area on each side (outside dimensions). Glue and nail these subroof sections in place. Then, just as for the siding, cut ⅛" × ¾" strips from ¾" wood. From these, cut 1" pieces for shingles. You can also make authentic-looking shingles by cutting ¾" × 1" pieces from cedar shakes.

Start at the bottom of the roofline, and work one row at a time. The first row of shingles is glued along the bottom of the subroof, but with each shingle extending over the edge by about ⅛". As you add each successive row of shingles, overlap the previous row again by about ⅛", staggering each row.

To make a flatter, stronger roof, use a strip of wood to clamp each new row as soon as it has been glued in place (Illus. 5). Give ample time for the row to dry, and then go on to start the next row.

Some of the house projects have extra touches, such as chimneys or porches, that can also be included as options for any of the

Illus. 5. Clamping shingles.

other houses. You will find directions for these options throughout the various projects. Use these options to encourage your creativity as you make each project design your own.

The choice of color for the structure is really a simple matter of individual preference, with perhaps some traditional or historical considerations. The colors given for each project or shown in the color photographs are only suggestions to help stimulate your own creative choices.

Inside walls should be painted or stained prior to the addition of the subroof. And often pieces such as chimneys or trim should be painted before they are actually glued in place.

The paints described throughout the book are acrylic folk art paints. These are available in either cans or plastic bottles. This type of paint is more fluid than tube paints and does not need to be watered down. For each particular project the colors suggested are muted colors.

If you would like an aged, peeling-paint sort of look for the clapboard siding, or even just for the shutters and trim or porch railings, you can achieve a very satisfying old "crackled" look using hide glue (Illus. 6). This is available in craft and hardware stores.

First brush the desired area with a thin layer of hide glue. Let this dry for about four hours.

Illus. 6. Wood on the left has been painted, wood on the right has been "crackled."

Then mix the acrylic paint with gesso (a form of base paint in use since at least the sixteenth century) in the proportion of two tablespoons gesso to one tablespoon of paint.

If you use more gesso proportionally, then the cracks will be smaller. Try some different test proportions to get the right amount of crackling for the look you want.

❖ Materials and Equipment ❖

This is a summary of the various materials and tools you will need to make the little houses and buildings in this book. The specific materials, with dimensions and quantities, and the necessary tools, with any accessories, are both listed at the start of each particular project.

MATERIALS

Wood

The basic construction for most of the miniature structures requires ¼″ wood. This, or any other, thickness of wood can be obtained by arranging to purchase ¾″ stock wood, then having it planed to the desired thickness by the lumber yard.

A very light and thin wood material, ⅛″ luan plywood, is used in the construction of sub-roofs and, in particular, the Barn roof.

The measurements given for the projects refer to the *actual measured thickness* of the wood; you should be aware that if you ask for a ¾″ board you will most likely be given something with an actual thickness of about ⅝″, and similarly a ½″ board will be more like ⅜″, and a 1″ board will be closer to ¾″. So be sure always to specify *actual measured thickness* or to know what standard lumber term it is that you will give you the thickness you actually need.

In only a few instances a board is identified by words, not numerals, as a two-by-four, a four-by-four, or a two-by ten. These names are not true thicknesses but are rough lumber dimensions before the board was planed.

Another option that you may want to consider is using plywood for the large ¼″ pieces. This might be a desirable material for this use, since ends won't show, the plywood won't split as easily, and it is usually economical.

Wooden Dowels

These round wooden sticks are used in various sizes for porch railings and as faux beams for the Mission Church. Larger diameter dowels also are used as logs for the Log Cabin.

Tin and Copper

Thin sheets of either tin or copper metal can be used for roofing. In this book, tin is used for the Farmhouse and Cottage, and copper is used for the roof of the turret for the Victorian house. Use tin snips or other metal cutters for proper cutting (Illus. 7).

Cedar Shakes

Cedar shingles that are used in roofing and sometimes siding for full-scale construction can be cut into ¾″ × 1″ pieces for the little houses. The thickness of the miniature shingles will vary, but it is precisely this variance that helps give your construction an authentic look. Precut miniature shingles can be purchased at many hobby and craft shops and stores selling materials for making dollhouses and miniatures.

Decorative Trim

Premade strips of decorative trim, ¹⁄₁₆″ to ⅛″ thick are generally available also at hobby and craft stores, especially those carrying dollhouse materials and other miniature accessories. Trim is used, in particular, for the Victorian House and the House with Picket Fence, and it can be used in place of cutting thin strips, as required, for house, door, window trim, and cross pieces.

Brass Bells

Available at most craft shops, these bells come in a variety of shapes and sizes. The size required for both churches is about ¾″ to 1″.

Illus. 7. Cutting tin with tin snips.

Sandpaper

Most sanding, whether by hand or by machine, requires medium-grade paper. However, final sanding should always be done by hand, with a fine-grade sandpaper.

Brads

These are very thin, finishing-type nails that work well when used in ¼″ wood (Illus. 8). They are available in various gauges and lengths.

Illus. 8. Use brads, plus glue, to join the walls.

Paint

The paints recommended for each project are acrylic folk art paints, which are available in cans or in plastic, upright containers. These paints are more fluid than tube paints and don't need to be watered down. Most colors are available already mixed to the sort of muted shades that are suggested for many of the constructions.

Stain

Stain is required to get the rustic weathered-log look for the Log Cabin and is suggested as an option for finishing the inside of the houses. It may also be used when a crackled effect is being used. In which case, you will want to be sure to stain the area first, let it dry, and then proceed with the glue and paint mixture (see page 11).

Gesso

This is a thick, base-coat paint, rather like a primer coat that artists use. Gesso can be purchased wherever artists' paints are sold. It is used to achieve an old crackled look as mentioned in the General Instructions.

Brushes

Use artist-quality brushes in ¼″, ½″, and 1″ sizes.

Wood Glue

Yellow wood glue, sometimes called carpenter's glue, or woodworking glue, should be used for all the steps where glue is required to bond pieces. Hold or clamp the glued sections together briefly if they are not going to be nailed immediately.

Hide Glue

This opaque glue is available at hardware and craft stores. Hide glue is sometimes referred to as traditional cabinetmaker's glue. It is used in these projects specifically to achieve the old crackled look. Allow the glue to dry completely before you paint over it.

Solder

When you are using tin to make a roof, it is necessary to solder the joints (Illus. 9). The same is also true for copper.

Emery Cloth

Use a fine emery cloth to sand any joints and surrounding areas that are to be soldered. This slight abrasion will make sure the surface is ready for soldering.

Hinges

Small, ¼″ hinges are required for the Barn and the House with Picket Fence. Use a jeweler's screwdriver to attach these tiny hinges.

EQUIPMENT

Goggles

Always wear some type of eye protection when you are cutting, sanding, or drilling.

Dust Mask

Wear a dust mask when you are sanding to avoid breathing in any fine particles. The same goes for sawing.

Illus. 9. *Soldering the joint of a tin roof.*

Tabletop Scroll Saw

A scroll saw, like a jigsaw, has a vibrating blade that moves up and down in a vertical position. It is extremely useful for small, intricate cuts and is needed to cut out the window openings for the houses (Illus. 10).

Band Saw

A band saw has a thin continuous blade that moves in one cutting direction (Illus. 11). It can make intricate cuts or saw through a four-by-four. Use a ⅛" blade for intricate work and a ¼" blade for straight cuts. This is a very versatile saw that can be used for all the cutting described in the book except for the window openings, which require the scroll saw.

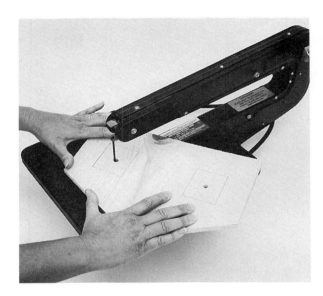

Illus. 10. Cut windows out with a scroll saw.

Radial-Arm Saw and Table Saw

Both of these saws use flat, circular blades available with various kinds of cutting teeth. While not able to do intricate cuts, these saws are good for precise "straight" cuts such as the basic cutting of wall or subroof pieces.

Sander

Use either a sanding disk or a small stationary belt sander as shown in Illus. 1. It is best to use medium-grade sandpaper with any of these machines.

Drill

Any portable hand drill is suitable. A variety of drill bits are necessary for the various projects and are identified as they are required.

Drill Press

This stationary drilling machine can be very helpful when you need it for achieving straight and accurate holes.

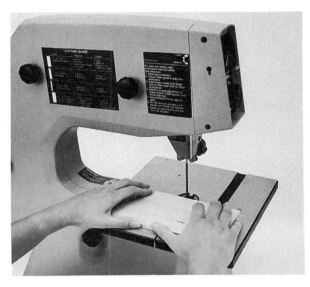

Illus. 11. A band saw is useful for both straight and curved cuts.

Hammer

Any small hammer or tack hammer will suffice for the projects in the book.

Jeweler's Screwdriver

Use this tiny screwdriver to fasten the hinges for the Barn and the House with Picket Fence.

Miniature Houses and Buildings

Whether you build one house or an entire village, these little houses will be cherished for decades to come. Not only can they be used as fine accent pieces or built as dollhouses or birdhouses, but also they can be incorporated into any holiday centerpiece, changing accessories just as you would with the home you live in.

They are especially attractive when used around New Year's and at Christmastime, along a mantel or under a tree. And a special charm is created when they are lit with miniature lights inside or out.

And they may be further put to use in their original calling as toy houses for play. Nowadays you might find little houses adorning a model railroad or a motorized miniature car track as much as the mantel or the middle of the holiday table. But certainly their value as gifts for display and as old-fashioned dollhouses will probably remain the greatest. These traditional uses endure.

FARM AND RANCH BUILDINGS

❖ Farmhouse ❖

This fundamental but pleasingly handsome little house is distinguished with its two chimneys. It can be made with or without shutters. The tin roof, made to resemble an old crimped, tin roof, may be painted with a green- or rust-colored wash for variety (Illus. 12). You also have the option of building the Farmhouse with a shingle roof.

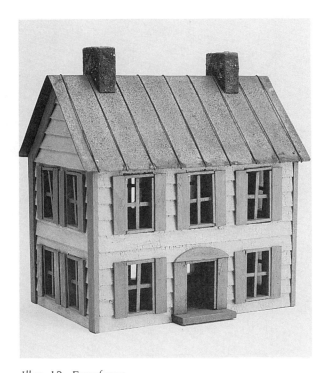

Illus. 12. Farmhouse

MATERIALS

Pine or plywood, ¼" thick, 5'
Pine, ½" thick, 8" × 24" (cut 12 pieces ⅛" × ½" × 24" for shutters, and window and peak trim)
Pine, ¾" thick, 10" × 16" (cut 24 pieces ¾" × ⅛" × 16" for siding)
Pine, ¾" thick, 1½" × 5" (chimney)
Pine, ¾" thick, 1" × 8" (roof support)
Tin, 10" × 10"
Wire, 18 gauge, 10'
Brads, ¾", No. 18, one box
Wood glue
Hide Glue
Gesso
Sandpaper
Stain, medium color
Acrylic paint: porcelain white, old ivy green (suggested)

TOOLS

Tabletop scroll saw
Band saw
Table saw
Tack hammer
Block plane (optional)
Drill
Drill bit, ½"
Paint brushes
Solder

Soldering iron
Tin snips
Pliers

INSTRUCTIONS

Basic Cutting

Using the dimensions given in Illus. 13, 14, and 15, cut the ¼" wood for the front, back, two sides, and the porch.

For the shutters, window, and peak trim, use a table saw to cut the ½" wood into twelve strips, ⅛" × ½" × 24". Also cut four strips, ¼" × ½" × 7", for the corner trim.

Then cut the ¾" wood into twenty-four strips, ¾" × ⅛" × 16". This will be used for the siding.

Windows

Draw the windows and door in place on all the main house sections: front, back, sides, etc. Then, using a ½" drill bit, drill a hole into the middle of each area to be cut out for windows. The door can be simply straight-cut, of course.

Disconnect the blade of the tabletop scroll saw, and slide the blade through one of the holes just drilled. Reattach the blade, and then carefully cut out the window. Repeat this procedure for each required opening.

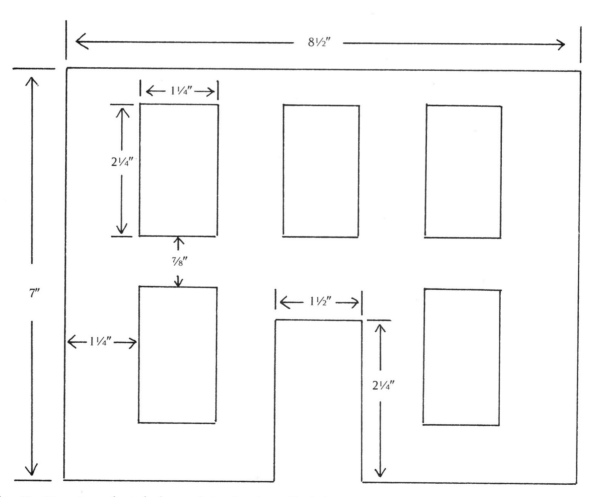

Illus. 13. Dimensions—front, back same but replace door with window.

House Assembly

Spread a thin bead of glue on the side edges of both side sections. Glue the house together so that the sides are inset into the front and back (Illus. 16). Then nail the joints together using several brads for each corner.

Once the glue has set, place the house on the remaining piece of ¼" wood, leaving an adequate length of scrapwood to cut the roof caps if you plan to build a shingle roof rather than the tin roof. Pencil along the inside perimeter of the house, and then cut out this section for the house base, or floor. Cut this

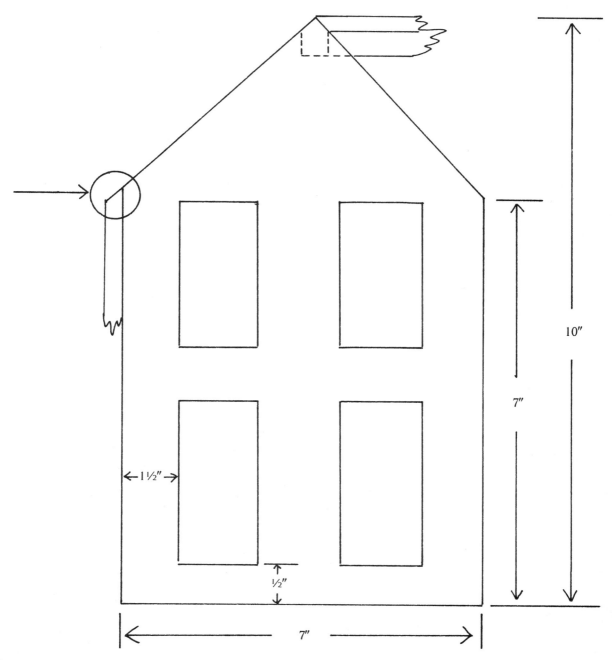

Illus. 14. Dimensions—side

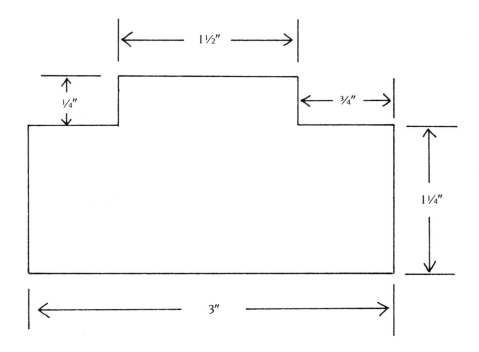

Illus. 15. Dimensions—porch

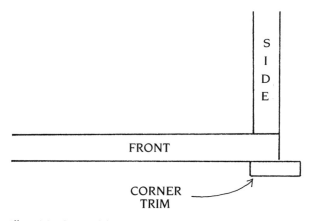

Illus. 16. Corner joint

carefully just to the outside of the pencil mark to ensure a good fit. Glue and nail this piece in place.

Stain, paint, or perhaps wallpaper the inside of the house at this point before you construct the roof.

Roof Support

Cut a roof support from ¾" wood. The finished support should measure ¾" × 1" × 8", but carefully measure the inside distance of the roof peaks between the side sections before cutting.

Using either a band saw or a block plane, trim along the top edges of the support to match the slope of the roof. Glue and nail the support into place.

Corner Trim

Attach the 7" lengths of corner trim as shown in Illus. 16. The trim should protrude beyond the side by ¼". Glue and nail the four pieces in place.

Window Frames

Cut, to fit, four pieces for each window frame from the ⅛" × ½" × 24" strips. When you are gluing the frames, be sure the inside edges of the pieces are flush with the inside walls. Glue only.

Siding

Starting from the bottom, measure and cut, to fit, pieces of siding from the previously cut twenty-four strips. As you work upwards, overlap each row by 1/8". Glue each one into place as you go.

Shutters and Peak Trim

Using the 1/2" × 1/8" strips, cut two shutters per window, to match the length of the windows. Also cut four pieces of peak trim to fit along the roof line.

For the tin roof the trim fits up against the tin under the overhang, whereas for the shingle roof the pieces are flush with the edge of the shingles and is topped by the roof cap as shown in Illus. 17. In either case mitre-cut the edges to be joined at the peak. Outline the door with this same trim, giving a rounded arch to the top edge of the door lintel piece.

Paint the shutters and trim before attaching them to the house.

Painting

To achieve an old crackled look, first apply hide glue with a brush to the entire house. Let this dry about 4 hours before painting. Mix acrylic paint with gesso (2 tablespoons gesso to 1 tablespoon paint). The more gesso you use the smaller the cracks will be.

For the siding an off-white color was used; for the trim a pale, grey-green was chosen. Since the selection of a color combination for paints and the choice of finishing technique are a matter of preference, you may find a great deal of satisfaction in using your own creativity here.

When the paint has dried thoroughly, glue the shutters and door trim in place, and then glue and nail the peak trim.

Roof

If you prefer to make the shingle roof, then follow the instructions for the Ranch House for the subroof and shingles (pages 38 and 40) adjusting for the Farmhouse dimensions.

To make the tin roof, use tin snips to cut a 10" × 10" piece of tin for the roof. Bend this piece in half to match the slope of the roof, then cut nine 11" pieces of wire.

Illus. 17. Peak trim

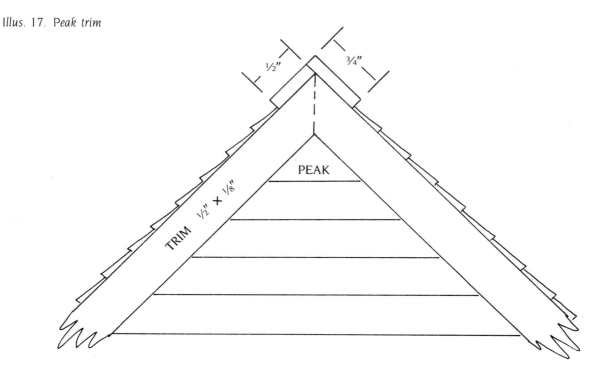

Bend each piece of wire in half, once again matching the roof angle. Evenly space the wires on the roof, then bend the ends under the roof edge using pliers. Solder the wires at the roof edges only. Tack roof into place (Illus. 18).

Chimney

Cut two chimneys from the ¾" wood to measure ¾" × 1½" × 1¾" (Illus. 19). Cut a "V" into the 1½" side to correspond with the angle of the roof. Glue the two chimneys in place on the roof cap, if you chose to make the shingled roof with the roof cap, or directly on the tin roof.

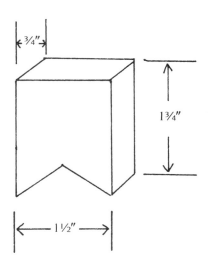

Illus. 19. *Chimney dimensions*

Illus. 18. *Tacking on roof.*

❖ 1900s Barn ❖

This reproduction of an antique toy barn features a hay loft, silos, and grooved doors that really open—a prized heirloom to be passed from generation to generation in your family (Illus. 20).

Pine, ¾″ × ¾″, 10′ length (ridge and braces)
Wood blocks, 1″ thick, 2½″ square, two (silo top)
   ¾″ thick, 1¼″ square, two (vents)

Illus. 20. Barn

MATERIALS

Pine, 3/16″ thick, 4″ × 24″ (cut 14 strips 3/16″ × 24″)
Pine, ¼″ thick, 12″ wide, 8 board feet (barn doors, etc.)
Pine, ½″ thick, 4″ × 28″ (silos)
Luan plywood, ⅛″ thick, 2′ × 2′ (roofing)

¾″ thick, ¾″ square, two (vents)
Wood dowel, ¼″ diameter, 8″ length
Hinges, ¼″, 6 sets
Brads, ¾″, No. 17, 1 box
Wood glue
Wood putty (nonshrinking)
Acrylic paint: white, red, blue-grey (suggested)

TOOLS

Tabletop scroll saw
Band saw
Table saw
Tack hammer
Drill
Circle-cutting bit, 2½"
Drill bit, ½"
Disk sander
Drill press
Carriage bolt and nut
Wood rasp
Brushes

INSTRUCTIONS

Basic Cutting

From the ¼" pine, cut the barn walls and base: front, 5½" × 22"; back, 5½" × 22"; two sides, 10" × 11"; and base, 9½" × 22".

Note that the sanding should be done prior to attaching any of the pieces throughout the project.

Doors and Windows

Draw the doors and windows on the barn wall pieces using the dimensions given in Illus. 21, 22, and 23. Cut out the doors, and then, using a ½" drill bit, drill a hole into the middle of the area where each window will be cut out.

Then, disconnect the blade of the tabletop scroll saw, and slide the blade through one of the holes. Reattach the blade, and then carefully cut out the window. Repeat this procedure for all of the remaining windows.

Basic Structure

First glue and nail the front and back sections to the base (Illus. 24), making sure the front, end door is to the left side. Then glue and nail the sides to the base; the door on the right side should be towards the back, the door on the left side towards the front.

Roof Ridges and Braces

The 1900s Barn has a gambrel roof, with a lower steeper slope and an upper flatter section on each of the two sides, that is particularly characteristic of the United States.

From the ¾" × ¾" wood, cut three roof ridges 22" long and two cross beams 9½" long. Glue and nail both of the cross beams into place. They are positioned 8" from each end, and flush with the top edge of the front and back wall sections.

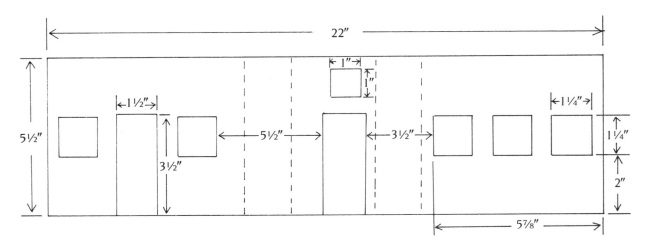

Illus. 21. Dimensions

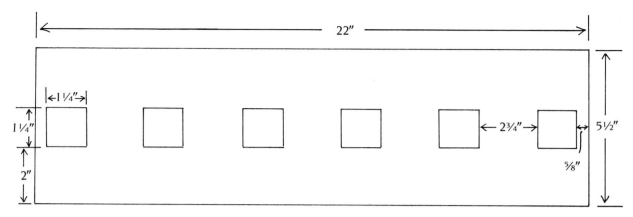

Illus. 22. Dimensions

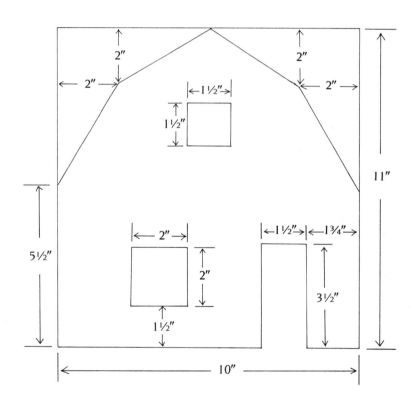

Illus. 23. Dimensions

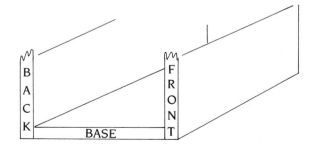

Illus. 24. Attaching front and back to base.

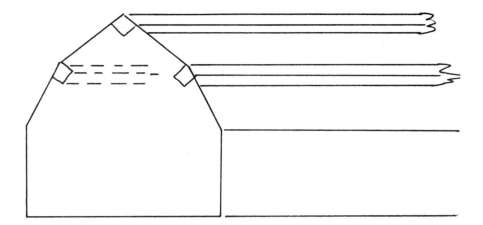

Illus. 25. Nail roof ridges at the
peaks.

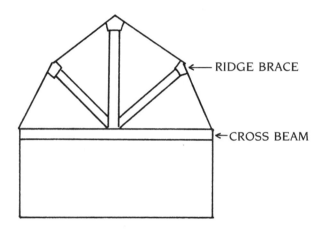

Illus. 26. Side view, cross beam,
ridge braces

Glue and then nail the three roof ridges for
the gambrel roof into place at each roof peak
as shown in Illus. 25.

Measure and cut, to fit, two sets of ridge
braces and glue into place as shown in Illus. 26.
There are one perpendicular and two angled
braces, providing a support for each cross
beam.

Roof

From ⅛″ luan plywood, cut two 4½″ × 24″
pieces and two 4″ × 24″ pieces.

Glue and nail into place the 4½″ pieces first,
starting at the lower roof peaks. Attach the 4″
pieces in the same manner, making sure they
meet at the top roof peak. The edges of the
lower roof will overlap the walls, and the edges

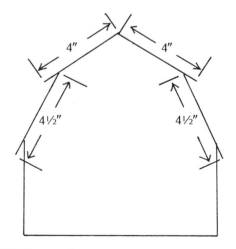

Illus. 27. Barn roof

of the upper roof will overlap the lower roof
sections (Illus. 27). Fill in the top seam with
wood putty as needed.

Dormers

To make the three dormers, first cut three triangular window sections from ¼" pine to the dimensions shown in Illus. 28. Drill a ½" hole into the section to be removed for the window. Using the scroll saw, cut out all of the window sections.

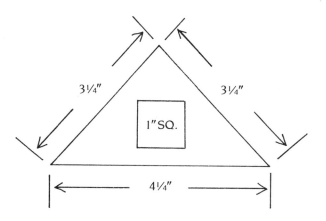

Illus. 28. Dimensions—dormers

From ⅛" luan plywood, cut six roof sections to the dimensions shown in Illus. 29.

Sand or cut the bottom edges of the three triangular ¼" pieces to match the slope of the roof sections. Glue the dormers together, and then glue one to the middle of the front lower roof section (just under the overlap). The remaining two should be glued equidistant between the middle dormer and the ends of the roof section.

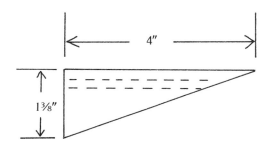

Illus. 29. Roof section

Door and Window Frames

From the ³⁄₁₆" strips cut, to fit, frames to go around all of the doors and windows. Then glue them into place, flush with the opening.

Cut a horizontal cross pane for each window. Then cut two vertical panes, and glue the pieces to form a cross. Insert the assemblies and glue them into the window openings.

Use two 22" strips and two 10⅜" strips for barn trim. Glue the trim ¼" above the top of the windows.

Measure the door openings, and cut both the small and large doors from ¼" pine. Groove the doors by using a carving tool or jackknife to give a planked look (Illus. 30).

Nail a medium-sized brad into each door to serve as a door knob. The brad should protrude about ⅛". Attach each door with two of the tiny hinges.

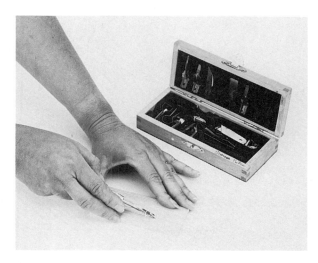

Illus. 30. Groove doors with a carving tool.

Vents

From ¾" wood, cut four blocks: two 1¼" square for the base of each vent, and two ¾" square to be moulded for the tops. Also cut two 1½" squares from ¼" wood.

Cut a "V", corresponding to the rooftop, into the 1¼" square blocks. Glue a 1½" square piece onto each of the base pieces, and then glue the ¾" squares on top.

32

Let the glue dry thoroughly, and then drill a hole into the middle of the top using a ³⁄₁₆" bit. Using a sanding wheel, sand the tops into a rounded pyramid shape.

Cut four 1¼" lengths of ³⁄₁₆" dowel. Shape these into "lightning rods" using a jackknife or carving tool. Glue a rod into the top of each vent to finish off the entire assembly (Illus. 31). Then glue these vents onto the roof. The remaining two lightning rods are for the silos.

Silos

To make the silos, first cut six 2" circles from ½" wood. Then from ⅛" wood, cut twenty-four strips ½" × 11" for the vertical siding of the silos.

Glue and nail the siding to the circles, placing three circles equidistant as shown in Illus. 32. Make sure the siding is flush with top and bottom.

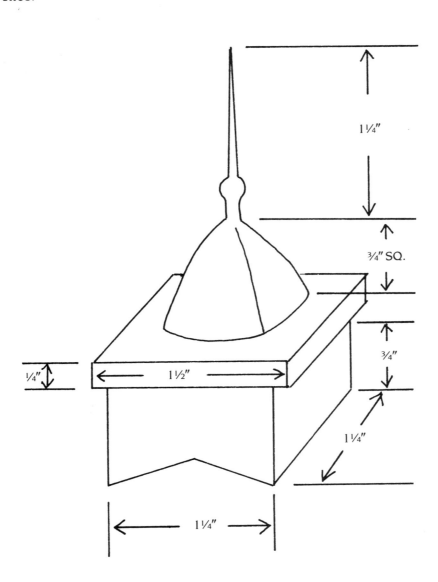

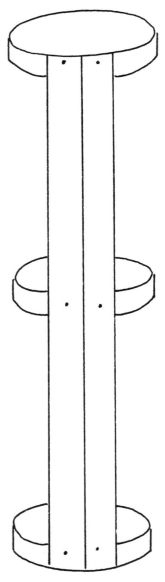

Illus. 32. Nail siding to wood circles to make the silos.

Illus. 31. Vent

For the top of each silo, cut two 2½" circles from 1" wood, using a circle-cutting bit/device on your drill. Make a hole in the middle of both circular pieces to fit the shaft of a carriage bolt.

Insert the carriage bolt into this hole in one of these circular pieces. Fasten the bolt tightly with a nut, and then insert the end of the bolt into the drill press.

With the drill turning the piece at high speed, shape the circle into a dome by using a wood rasp and sandpaper (Illus. 33). Glue the dome to the top of the silo. Use the drill to expand the hole to ³⁄₁₆" in the top of each dome, then attach the lightning rods.

Painting

Use white acrylic paint for the barn sides, front and back (above the trim), the silos, roof vents, and all trim and doors.

Paint below the trim line with a dark red. When this is completely dry, paint thin white lines to create the look of brick wall.

Paint the gambrel roof a blue-grey color.

Illus. 33. *Making the dome for the silo.*

❖ Ranch ❖

This little one-storey ranch house features a wraparound porch on three sides and a hip roof (Illus. 34). Some of the charming details you can add on your own are a corner porch swing, a mounted flag pole on the front porch column, and even miniature flower pots to decorate the windows.

Wood, ½" thick, 8" × 14"
Wood, ¾" thick, 8" × 24"
Wood two-by-four, 2½" length (chimney)
Wood dowel, ⅛" diameter, 36" length, three
Luan plywood, ⅛" thick, 2' × 4'
Cedar shakes (to cover roof area)
Wood glue

Illus. 34. Ranch

MATERIALS

Wood, ¼" thick, 10" × 6'
Wood, ⅜" square, 6'

Hide glue
Sandpaper
Brads, ¾", No. 18, one box
Acrylic paint: off-white, slate blue, brick red

TOOLS

Table saw or radial-arm saw
Tabletop scroll saw
Drill with ½″ and ⅛″ bits
Tack hammer
Paint brushes

INSTRUCTIONS

Basic Cutting

From ¼″ wood, cut the base, front, back, and two sides to the dimensions given in Illus. 35, 36, and 37. Also cut 6′ of ⅛″ strips; these can be cut as four 18″ lengths. You will use these later to make the porch railings.

For trim and shutters use ½″ wood, and cut ten ⅛″ × 14″ strips.

Windows and Doors

Consult Illus. 35, 36, and 37 for the placement and measurement of the windows and doors. Draw these in place; then, using the ½″ bit, drill a hole through the middle of each drawn window.

Use the tabletop scroll saw to cut out the windows. First detach the blade, and insert it into one of the holes; then reattach the blade.

Make preliminary cuts to the corners, backing up to the middle after each cut, for ease in cutting out the windows (Illus. 38). Repeat this procedure for each window, and then cut out the doors.

House Assembly and Trim

Glue and nail the sides to the front and back sections. Then from the ⅛″ × ½″ × 14″ strips cut, to fit, trim for all of the windows and doors. Glue the trim pieces in place so that their inside edges are flush with the inside walls.

From these same strips, cut four 5″ pieces for corner trim. Glue these to the sides so that they protrude to the front (or back) about ¼″.

There will be a space above the corner trim to the top of the wall since the walls are 5½″ high; however, this will serve as a stop guide for finishing the siding. This is important because the space is needed for anchoring the rafters to the top of the walls.

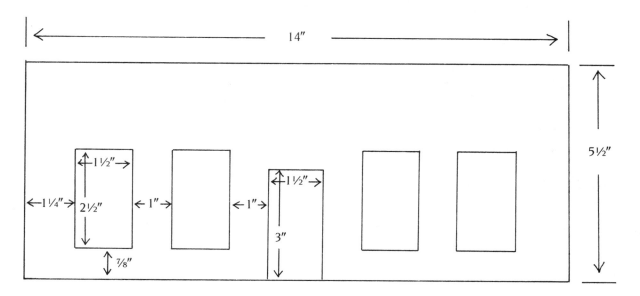

Illus. 35. Dimensions—front

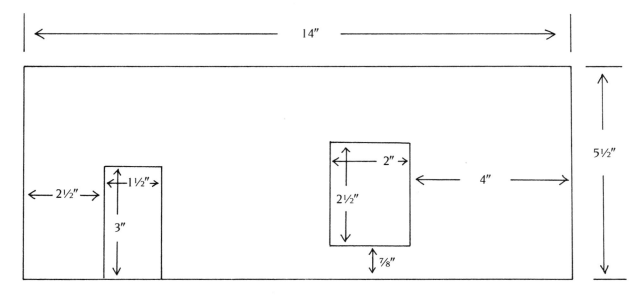

Illus. 36. Dimensions—back

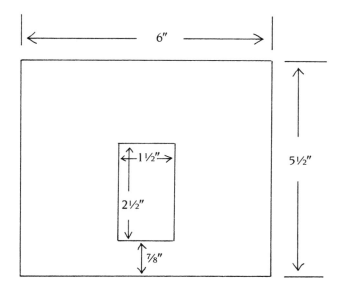

Illus. 37. Dimensions—side

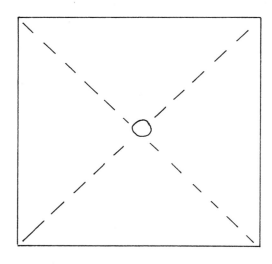

Illus. 38. Make cuts to the corners of the windows.

Roof Rafters

Using ¾" wood again, cut strips ¼" × ¾" for the following roof supports: one top (main), 8¼"; two sides, 5"; four corners, 6"; three front, 5½"; and three back, 5½".

Each support, with the exception of the main piece, will need to have one end cut at an angle, to fit flush with the main piece. These will also have to be notched to fit the top of the walls (Illus. 39).

Starting approximately one inch from the end of the 5" side supports, cut out a notch to fit the shape of the wall. Position these supports at such an angle so that there is a 8¼" space between them to attach the main support piece as indicated in Illus. 39.

Glue and nail the side roof supports to the top of the side walls at the midpoint, equidis-

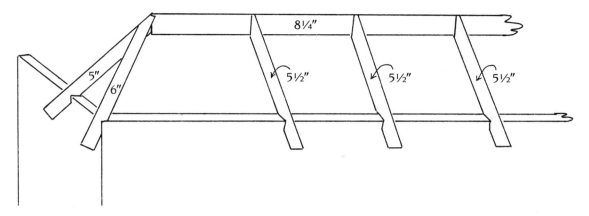

Illus. 39. Roof ridge—rafters

tant from each corner. Then glue the main support in place. Attach the front and back supports in the same manner, spacing them equally along the main piece.

Notch and angle the 6" corner pieces, and glue and nail them to the corners.

Siding and Shutters

To make the siding, cut twenty-two 14" strips ⅛" × ¾" using the ¾" thick wood. Cut each piece to fit as you progress from the bottom to the top. Glue the first piece in place flush with the bottom, working on one side at a time.

As you work upwards, overlap each row ⅛" and glue in place, but remember to stop ½" from the top. Using these same strips, cut two shutters for each window to match the length of the window. Glue the shutters in place.

Now you are ready to stain or paint the inside of the house and the base. Then glue and nail the house to the base. The house should be positioned on the base with the back of the house and back of the base flush, and with the sides of the house equidistant from the side edges of the base.

Porch Supports, Rafters, and Railings

From a length of ⅜" × ⅜" wood, cut six 4" posts. Glue these in place, one at each corner (⅛" from base edges) and two in front of the

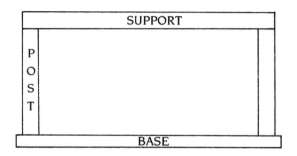

Illus. 40. Nail supports on top of the porch posts.

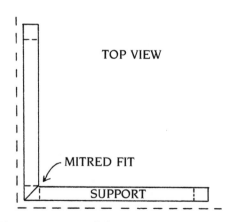

Illus. 41. Mitre corners of the supports where they meet.

door (2¼" apart). Also cut the porch roof supports from this ⅜" × ⅜" piece: one, 19⅜" (front) and two, 9⅜" (sides).

Glue and nail the supports on top of the posts (Illus. 40). Mitre the corners where the supports join and rest on a post (Illus. 41).

38

Using ½" wood, cut ¼" × ½" strips for the porch rafters. You will need: three front, 4"; four side, 3½"; two corner, 5¼".

Notch and angle these in the same manner as the roof rafters. Position these rafters next to the existing roof rafters, then glue and nail them into place (Illus. 42).

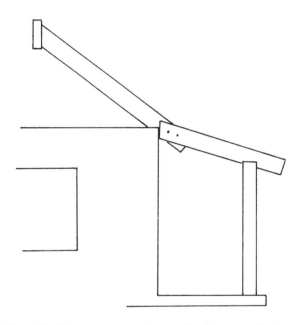

Illus. 42. Side view, connecting porch rafters to roof rafters.

To make the upper and lower railings, cut four 18" strips ⅛" × ¼" from ¼" wood. Place two strips together and tack a brad into each end to hold them securely.

With a ⅛" bit, drill a hole at each ½" interval. Repeat this procedure for the other set of strips. Cut a 7⅝" and a 8½" piece from each strip.

Now cut sixty-four 1¼" pieces from the ⅛" dowels. Separate the railings, and then glue and insert the 1¼" dowel pieces to make the porch railings.

Set the porch railings aside until the outside of the house has been painted.

Subroof

The Ranch House has a hip roof, which has sloping ends and sloping sides. Connected to this is a porch roof that extends over the porch.

For the subroof, cut, from ⅛" plywood, a front, back, and two sides for the hip roof, and also cut a front and two sides for the porch roof. Follow the dimensions given in Illus. 43, 44, 45, 46, and 47. Glue and then nail the front section and the back section in place for the main subroof.

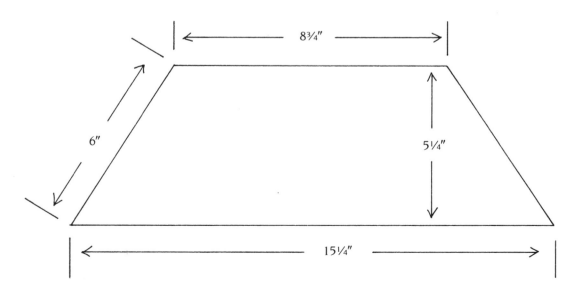

Illus. 43. Subroof—front

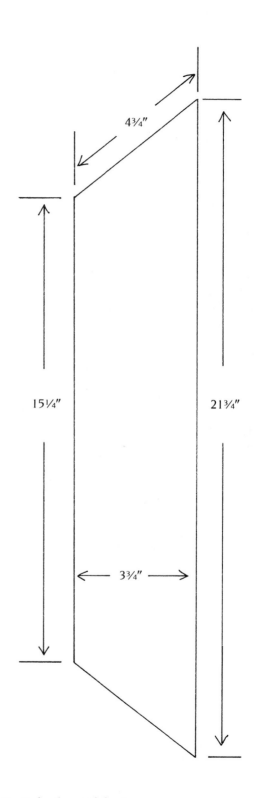

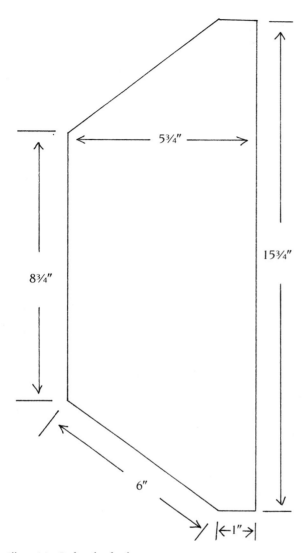

5¾″

8¾″

15¾″

6″

|←1″→|

Illus. 44. Subroof—back

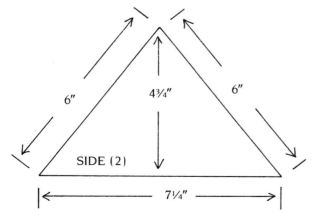

6″

4¾″

6″

SIDE (2)

7¼″

Illus. 45. Subroof—side

4¾″

15¼″

21¾″

3¾″

Illus. 46. Subroof—porch front

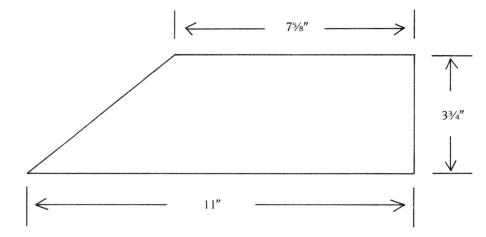

Illus. 47. Subroof—porch side

Be sure to check the dimensions of your structure to see if any slight corrections are needed for the side subroof dimensions. Attach the side pieces, and then, making the seams as flush as possible, glue and nail the porch subroof in place.

Shingles

Use cedar shakes to cut 1½″ × 1½″ squares for the shingles. Cut to fit at the corners and seam lines.

Starting from the bottom, glue a row of shingles in place; then, overlapping ¼″ glue on the next row, stagger placement by about half the shingle width for each row. If necessary, clamp a strip of wood across each row as it is glued to hold the shingles securely in place until they dry. This procedure is more time consuming, but it does make a sturdier, flatter roof.

When you have finished covering the roof, cut a roof cap ¼″ × ¾″ × 9½″ from ¾″ wood. Glue and nail this piece on top of the roof line.

From ⅛″ plywood, cut two ½″ × 5¼″ strips and four ½″ × 6″ strips. Use these to trim the seam lines of the roof. The 6″ strips are used for the hip roof, and the 5¼″ strips for the porch roof.

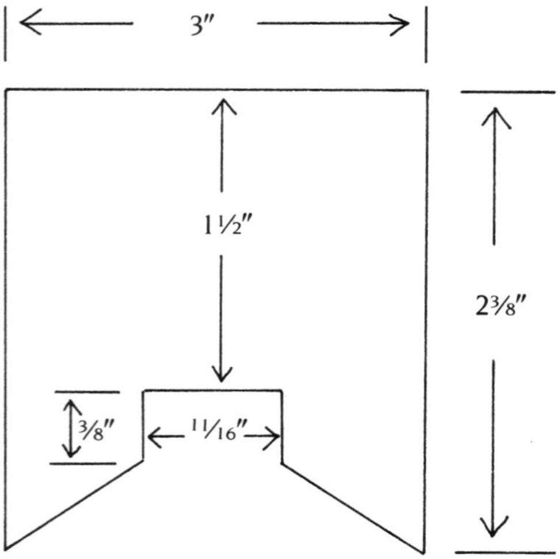

Chimney

From a piece of two-by-four wood, cut a 2″ × 2½″ block for the chimney. Cut out a section to correspond to the roof line (Illus. 48), and then glue into place.

Painting

Paint the trim, roof, porch railings, and posts with an off-white color. Slate blue is suggested for the house siding. Chimney, shutters, and the porch floor are a brick red color.

Porch railings can give an extra aged charm if you paint them with the crackled finish (see the General Instructions and also page 25).

Illus. 48. Chimney

HISTORIC BUILDINGS

❖ Log Cabin ❖

This rustic little log cabin is built from wood dowels—a perfect addition to a little house collection (Illus. 49). Its handsome weathered wood look and the many rich details like the "stone" chimney, windows, and intersecting corner logs help capture the frontier spirit of the settlers.

MATERIALS

Pine, ½" thick, 10" × 28"
Pine, ¼" thick, 10" × 15½"
Pine, ⅝" thick, ⅝" × 17½" strip
Wood two-by-four, one 13" length
Barn wood, ½" thick, 6" × 6' (or other ½" wood)

Illus. 49. Log Cabin

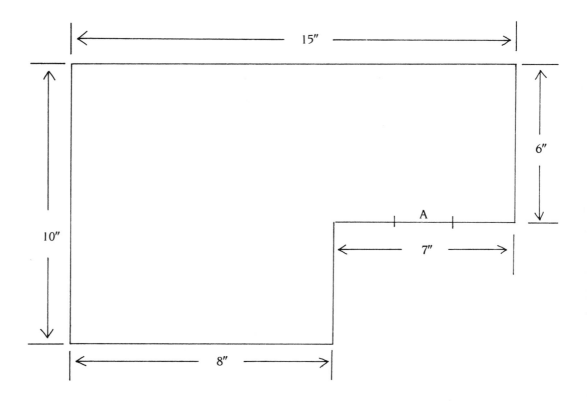

Illus. 50. Base for the log cabin

Wood dowels, ⅜″ diameter × 36″, four
Wood dowels, ½″ diameter × 36″, twenty-two
Wood dowel, ¼″ diameter, 1¼ length, one only
Brads, ¾″, No. 17, one box
Stain, 1 pint
Paint, light grey (suggested for the roof if barn
    wood is unavailable)
Sand, 1 oz
Wood glue

TOOLS

Band saw
Table saw
Tack hammer
Penknife
Drill with ¼″ bit

INSTRUCTIONS

Base and Door Frames

From ½″ pine, cut one base piece to the dimensions given in Illus. 50. Also cut six strips, ¼″ × 12″, to be used for the door and window frames (Illus. 51).

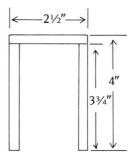

Illus. 51. Door frame

From the strips cut two 3¾" pieces and one 2½" piece for the door frame. Glue and nail the frame in position adjacent to what is labelled wall A in Illus. 50 since the logs will be built up from the outside of the base edge. Make sure that the corners of the frame are square, and that the door is positioned along the 7" edge of the base right in the middle of what will become wall A.

Walls

For the first row of logs, cut seven pieces of ½" dowel to these lengths: one 2¼", one 3½," one 3¾", one 6", one 10", one 11", and one 18". Full-length logs that extend beyond the intersecting wall will be 3" longer than the corresponding base measurement.

Glue and nail the logs to the *SIDE* of the base as shown in Illus. 52. The logs that are longer than the corner will extend 1½" beyond the adjacent wall.

For the second row, again cut seven pieces but to these lengths: one 1¾", one 2¼", one 5½", one 8", one 9", one 13", and one 15". Glue and nail these logs on top of the base row.

Alternate sizes (identical to the first row, and then the second row) until you have completed the fifth row on which the window frames will sit.

Window Frames

From ½" pine, cut six strips ¼" × 12". Then cut pieces from these strips to the appropriate lengths for each window.

The front window requires two 1½" pieces and two 4" pieces. For the remaining five windows you will need to cut ten 2" pieces and ten 2½" pieces.

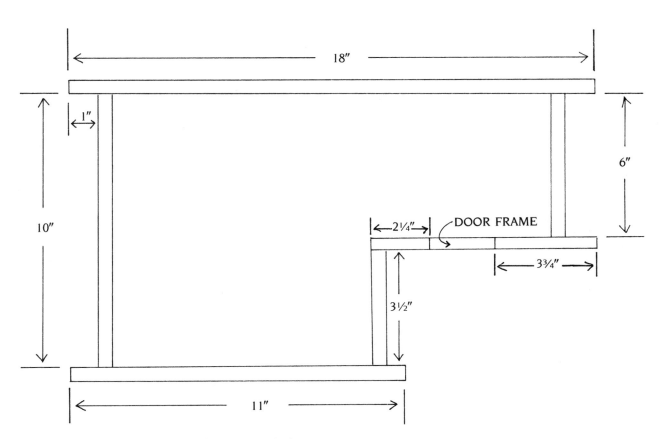

Illus. 52. Glue and nail the logs to the "sides" of the base.

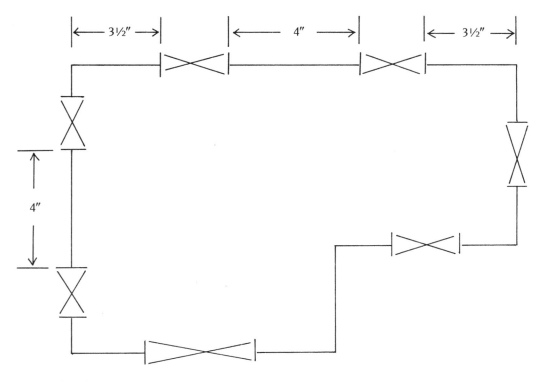

Illus. 53. Position of windows

Glue and nail each window frame, making sure that the corners are perfectly square. The outside dimensions of the window frames are 2″ × 4″ for the front and 2½″ × 2½″ for the side and back.

The exact placement of the windows is diagrammed in Illus. 53. Glue each window frame securely in place. Be sure to leave 4″ between the two side windows on the longest side wall to allow for the chimney.

Add five more rows of logs, one row at a time. Cut the logs to fit the spaces both between and beside the window frames. Notch out the logs that extend across the top of the window frames if the logs are not exactly flush with the top of the frame.

Foundation and Porch

After you have reached the tenth row of logs, add the porch and foundation.

From ¼″ pine, cut three strips 1″ × 15½″, and also cut out a 5″ × 7½″ porch floor. Also cut a 5″ length of ½″ dowel for the porch corner post, which acts as a roof support.

Now cut three foundation sections from the 1″ strips to these lengths: one 5″, one 8¼″, and one 8½″; and for the fourth foundation section use one strip that remains 15½″.

Glue and nail the four foundation pieces and the porch floor to the base of the cabin (Illus. 54). The strips will overlap part of each log (Illus. 55).

From ½″ wood cut a front door step to measurements shown (Illus. 56). Attach the step to the door frame with glue.

Glue the corner post in position making sure it is straight. Then add one more row of logs, the eleventh, with the front log extending over the porch post.

Ridge Braces

Cut two 9½″ ridge braces from ⅜″ thick dowels. Also cut a 15″ length for the roof ridge.

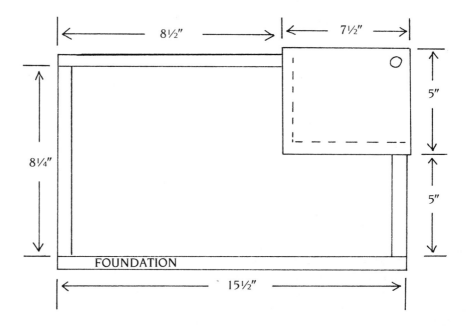

Illus. 54. Bottom view,
foundation

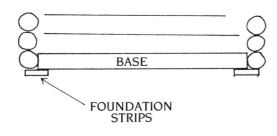

BASE

FOUNDATION
STRIPS

Illus. 55. Side view

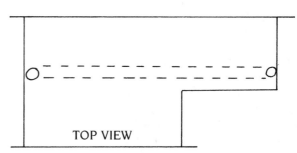

TOP VIEW

Illus. 57. Glue and nail ridge braces against side cabin
walls.

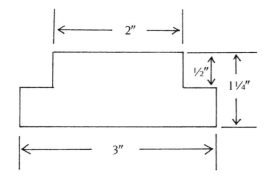

Illus. 56. Front door step

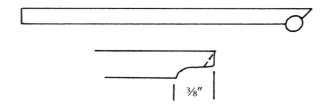

Illus. 58. Cut a notch into each rafter.

Roof Rafters

From the ⅜″ dowels, cut eighteen 9″ roof
rafters. Cut a notch into one end of each rafter
(Illus. 58).

Glue and nail the braces inside of the cabin,
making sure they are plumb (Illus. 57). Glue
and nail the roof ridge in place.

Glue and nail the rafters at each end of the
cabin (Illus. 59). Then, in the remaining space,

48

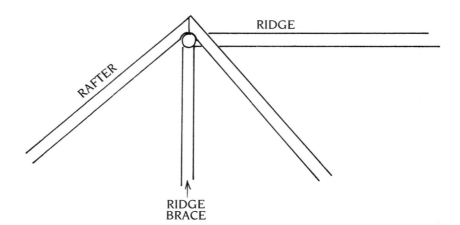

Illus. 59. Roof ridge—end rafters

position and fasten the other 14 rafters, equally spaced, approximately 2" apart.

Finish adding logs to the side walls of the cabin, cutting to fit the angle of the roofline (Illus. 60). Ends can be sanded for a snug fit.

Chimney

To make the chimney, cut the two-by-four to the dimensions given in Illus. 61. With the band saw, make horizontal 1/16" deep, random cuts on the front, sides, and three inches down the back. Use a jackknife or carving tool to make vertical cuts to resemble a stone or brick chimney.

Prepare for attaching the chimney by first drilling a 1/4" hole into the chimney back, approximately 4" from the bottom. Glue and insert the 1/4" diameter dowel (Illus. 62). Drill a corresponding hole into the cabin wall. (Do not attach the chimney until the next step is completed.)

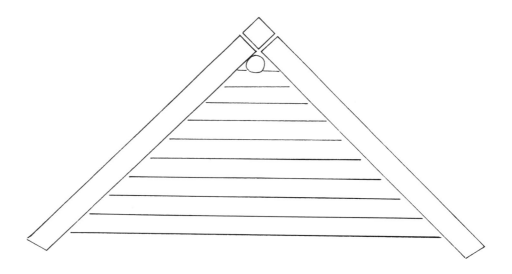

ENDS OF LOGS MATCH ROOF ANGLE

LOG

Illus. 60. Taper logs to form the roof peak.

32

Staining and Painting

Using either a rag or a brush, stain the inside and outside of the log cabin. Wipe off any excess stain to be sure you'll have a uniform finish.

Paint the chimney with a base coat of grey paint. As this dries, mix a small amount of sand with some grey paint. The mixture should be slightly gritty. Dab this mixture on the drying paint with your fingers. Apply to the front, sides, and the top three inches of the chimney back. Set aside to dry.

Glue the chimney in place when it is completely dry. Make sure it is evenly positioned at the peak.

Roof

From the ½" barn wood, or any other ½" wood, cut six 6" × 8½" roof sections. Notch out two of the sections so that they fit snugly around the chimney. Nail all the sections in place, attaching them to the rafters.

Using ⅝" wood, cut a ⅝" × ⅝" strip that is 17½" long for the roof cap. Glue this in place at the top of the roof line.

If you are using wood other than barn wood, stain the roof a barn-wood grey color or paint it with a thin wash of grey paint (diluted paint). You might want to stain or paint the exposed cut edges of the roof wood even if you have some aged barn wood to work with.

Illus. 61. Dimensions of chimney

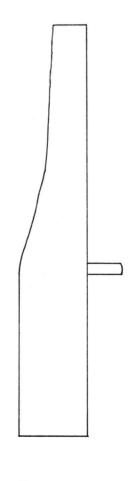

Illus. 62. Side view, chimney

❖ Rex Theatre ❖

The Rex—a must for all house collectors—is reminiscent of the old-time movie theatres (Illus. 63). The wood used for the theatre pictured was weathered barn wood; however, any wood of the proper thicknesses may be used and then stained with a barn-wood grey color. This project would also be quite eye-catching if it were painted in contrasting colors, perhaps a combination of forest green, mustard gold, and tan.

Illus. 63. Rex Theatre

MATERIALS

Wood, ¾″ thick, 12″ × 2′
Wood, ½″ thick, 10″ × 8′
Wood, ⅝″ thick, 8″ × 2½′
Wood, ¼″ thick, 8″ × 12″
Wood, ⅛″ thick, 6″ × 10″
Wood dowel, ¼″ diameter
Plexiglas, 1⁄16″ thick, 4″ × 5″
Brads, 1″, No. 18, one box
Wood glue
Sandpaper
Barn-wood grey stain (optional)
Acrylic paint: ivory, light green, brick (suggested)

TOOLS

Tabletop scroll saw
Table or radial-arm saw
Tack hammer
Drill with ½″ bit and ¼″ bit
Paint brush

INSTRUCTIONS

Basic Cutting

Using either a table saw or radial-arm saw, cut two strips from the ¾″ wood, ⅛″ × 14″. Set these aside to use later as trim for the entrance overhang. Now cut the base piece, 9½″ × 13″, also from the ¾″ wood.

From the ½″ wood, cut two sides, 8½″ × 9½″, and one back, 9″ × 12″. Cut off the top corners of the back following the dimensions in Illus. 64. Then cut the front roof support to the shape and dimensions shown in Illus. 65.

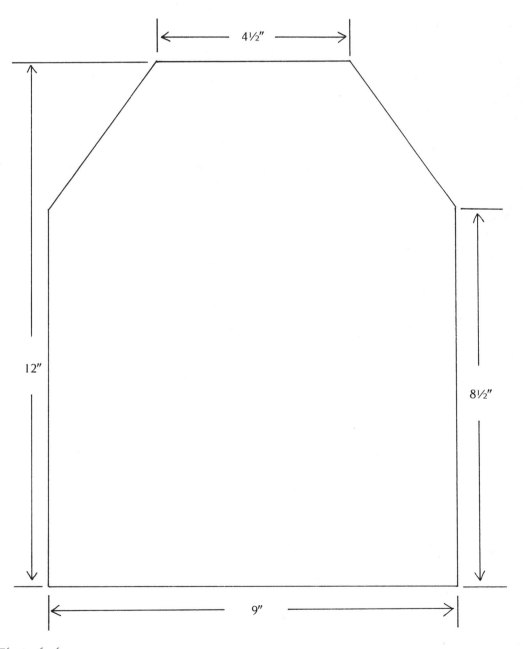

Illus. 64. Theatre back

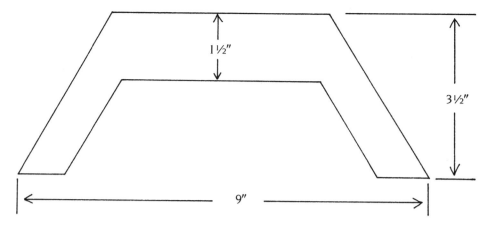

1½"

3½"

9"

Illus. 65. Front roof support

Roof sections may be cut at this time as well; cut a top section, 5" × 10½", and also cut two side sections, 4¾" × 10½".

Main Structure

Glue and nail the sides to the back, keeping the corners square (Illus. 66). Then, glue and nail the front roof support to the sides.

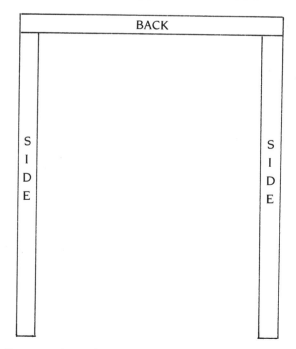

BACK

SIDE

SIDE

Illus. 66. Glue and nail the sides to the back, keeping the corners square.

Roof

Attach the top roof section so that it is flush with the front. Glue and nail it in place, making sure that it is positioned properly in the middle. Glue and nail the side roof sections in place, also making sure that they are flush with the front.

Now you can fasten the base piece to the structure with glue and nails. The back and sides of the theatre should set approximately ¼" from the edges.

Front Entrance

From ⅝" wood, cut two front pieces, 2" × 6¼". Notch out one corner to the measurements shown in Illus. 67.

Glue and nail these front pieces to the sides. The notched sections will extend over the base piece as you can see in Illus. 63.

Cut two pieces, 3⅝" × 5½", and another piece, 5¼" × 5½", from the ¼" wood. Cut two door openings in the larger piece to the dimensions in Illus. 68. Sand the side edges of this piece at an angle to fit the side pieces as shown in Illus. 69.

The edges of the side pieces that meet the front section will also need to be sanded at an angle. Glue these three pieces together to form the entrance.

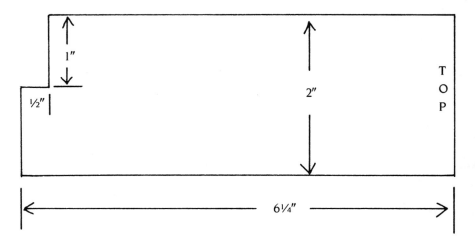

Illus. 67. *First floor fronts—cut two.*

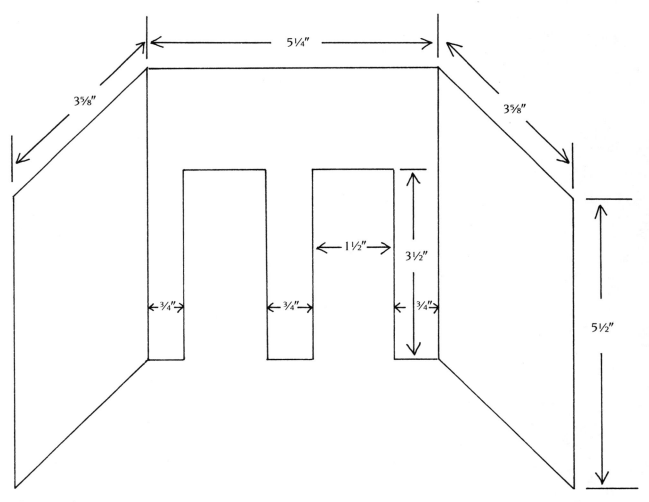

Illus. 68. *Theatre entrance*

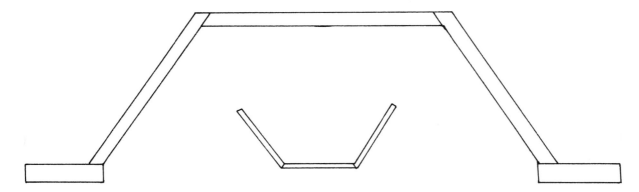

Illus. 69. Top view, entrance

Ticket Booth

Using a scroll saw or band saw, cut two sides, 1⅝" × 5⅜", and one front, 1½" × 5⅜", from ⅛" wood. Cut the top and bottom to the shape and dimensions shown in Illus. 70. Also cut a center support to the same dimensions as the top and bottom but following the shape given in Illus. 71.

Illus. 71. Center support

Draw the windows, and then drill a hole into each window section. Detach the scroll saw blade, and insert the saw blade through one of the holes. Reattach the blade, and cut out the window area. Use this procedure to cut out the two remaining windows.

Sand the side edges of the ticket booth pieces so that they will join in a mitred fit (Illus. 72). Glue these pieces together, fitting the top and bottom in place.

Illus. 70. Ticket booth

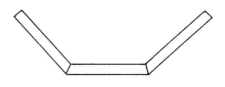

Illus. 72. Top view, ticket booth (mitred fit)

Using the band saw, cut three pieces of ¹⁄₁₆″ Plexiglas, slightly wider than each window opening and approximately ⅜″ longer. Glue these windows inside the booth, and then glue the center support just beneath the bottom edge of the windows.

Spread glue on the bottom of the ticket booth once all joints have dried, and attach the booth to the base. The ticket booth should jut forward approximately ½″ more than the sides of the front section.

Entrance Overhang

For the entrance overhang and ceiling, from ½″ wood, cut a 6¾″ × 9¼″ piece. Then cut out the ½″ notched sections as shown in Illus. 73.

Glue and nail this piece in place so that it rests level, horizontally, on the entrance walls.

Front and Windows

From the remaining ⅝″ wood, cut two ⁵⁄₁₆″ × 12″ strips. Cut these into four 2¼″ pieces and four 3″ pieces. Glue and nail these to make the window frames.

Cut twelve ⅝″ × ⅝″ strips to finish the front; then cut to required sizes shown in Illus. 74. Also cut two small pieces to fit next to the entrance overhang—they should fit flush with the sides. First glue and nail these two pieces in place.

Glue and nail the 11″ piece next, above the overhang. For the next row glue and nail a 2½″ strip, a window, a 1½″ strip, a window, and a 2½″ strip. Continue to build the front wall in this manner, following the pattern of Illus. 74.

For window crosspieces, cut a 12″ length of a ¼″ × ¼″ strip. Then cut, to fit, crosspieces, and glue them into place.

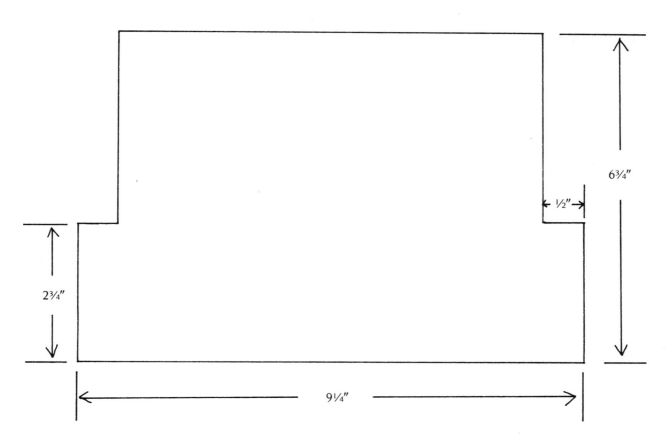

Illus. 73. Entrance overhang

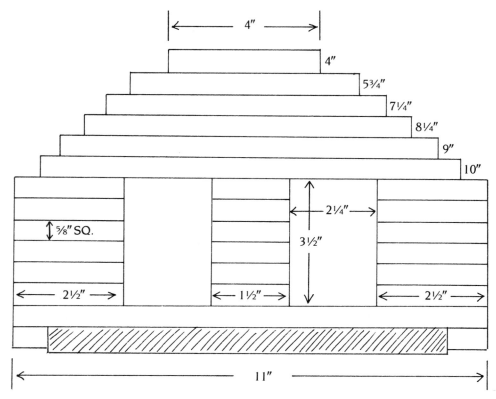

Illus. 74. Front, second storey

Theatre Sign

From ½" wood, cut a 1¾" × 6¾" piece. Round the top corners, using a band saw or a sander, to match the shape in Illus. 75.

Drill two ¼" holes into one side, positioning one about 1½" from the top and the other about 1½" from the bottom. Drill the holes to a depth of approximately ½".

Cut two ¼" thick dowel pieces 1¼" long. Insert these into the holes, and use the projecting ends to determine the placement of holes in the theatre front. The sign piece should be positioned midway between the windows and ¼" above the entrance overhang. Then drill the holes approximately ½" deep. Glue the sign and dowels into place.

On ⅛" wood, draw the letters "REX" twice. These letters should be approximately 1¼" wide and 1½" high. Cut out with either a scroll saw or band saw, using a fine-tooth blade.

Glue the letters to both sides of the sign.

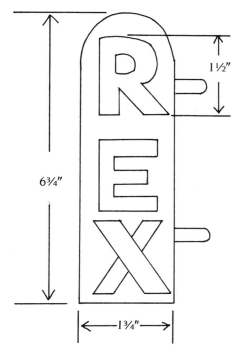

Illus. 75. Rex Theatre sign

Trim

From a ¾″ scrap, cut one ⅛″ × 9½″ strip and two ⅛″ × 2″ strips. Glue and nail these strips to the front and side edges of the entrance overhang.

An optional detail that you may enjoy adding to give an extra feeling of authenticity is to rip small pieces from a newspaper movie section, and then glue a few scraps to both sides of the front to look like old billboards.

Painting

Paint the sign letters and the entrance walls an off-white. To match the old weathered painted boards used, the ticket booth is painted light green on the bottom half, but brick red on the top half.

MATERIALS

Wood, ¼" thick, 10" × 5½'
Wood, ⅜" square, 4'
Wood, ½" thick, 10" × 3'
Wood, ¾" thick, 12" × 3½' (Roof caps, shingles, and siding)
Plywood, ⅛" thick, 2' × 2'
Decorative trim, 1/16" thick, ½" × 5'
Copper 0.025 gauge, 5" × 6"
Wood dowel, ⅛" diameter, two 36" lengths
Emery paper, small pieces
Wood glue
Epoxy
Brads, ¾", No. 18, one box
Acrylic paint: off-white, gold ochre, dark green, brick red (suggested)
Stain: medium color

TOOLS

Table, radial-arm, or band saw
Tabletop scroll saw
Tack hammer
Drill with ⅛" and ½" bits
Soldering iron and solder
Metal cutters or tin snips
Flat-end pliers (linesman's)

INSTRUCTIONS

Basic Cutting

Following the dimensions in Illus. 77 through Illus. 82, cut house pieces and an 11¼" × 15½" base from ¼" wood. Note the identification of

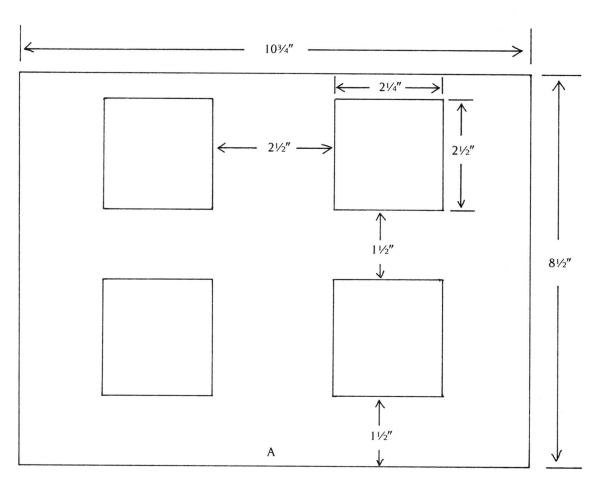

Illus. 77. Wall A

60

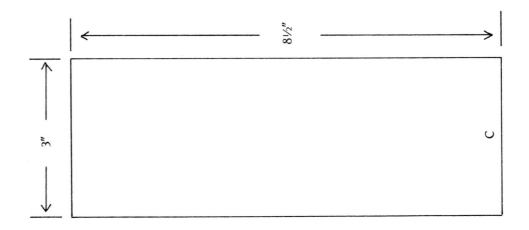

Illus. 79. Wall C

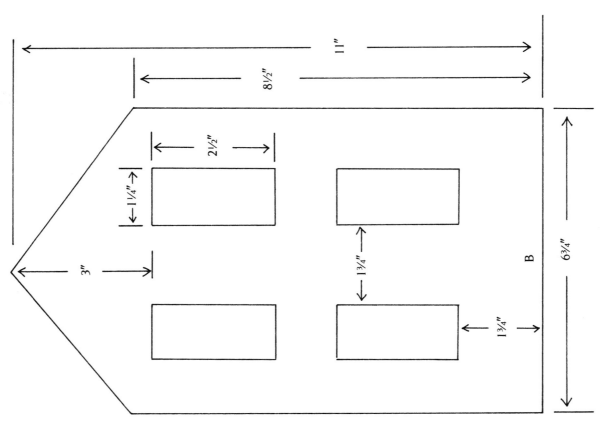

Illus. 78. Wall B

61

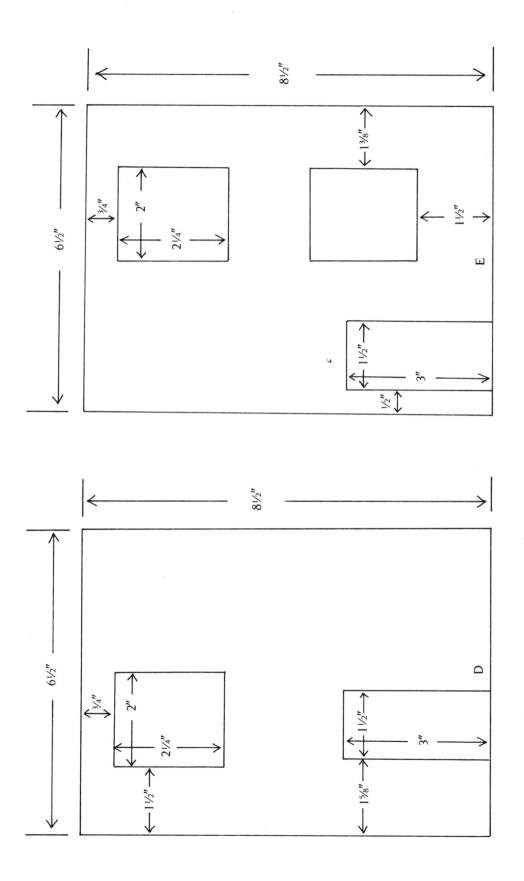

Illus. 81. Wall E

Illus. 80. Wall D

each section, A through F. You will need two C sections and two B sections. Also cut three 1¼″ × 8½″ pieces for the turret (Illus. 83).

From ⅛″ wood, cut out the subroof sections for the house and the porch a shown in Illus. 84, 85, 86, and 87. Do not notch the roof sections until they can be fitted to the turret.

Windows and Doors

Draw the windows and doors onto the house and turret sections. Consult the appropriate diagrams for their dimensions and placement.

With a ½″ bit, drill a hole into the middle of each area where a window is drawn. Using a tabletop scroll saw, cut out the windows. Do this by detaching the blade and inserting it into one of the holes. Then reattach the blade. Make preliminary cuts from the hole to the corners for ease in cutting out the window.

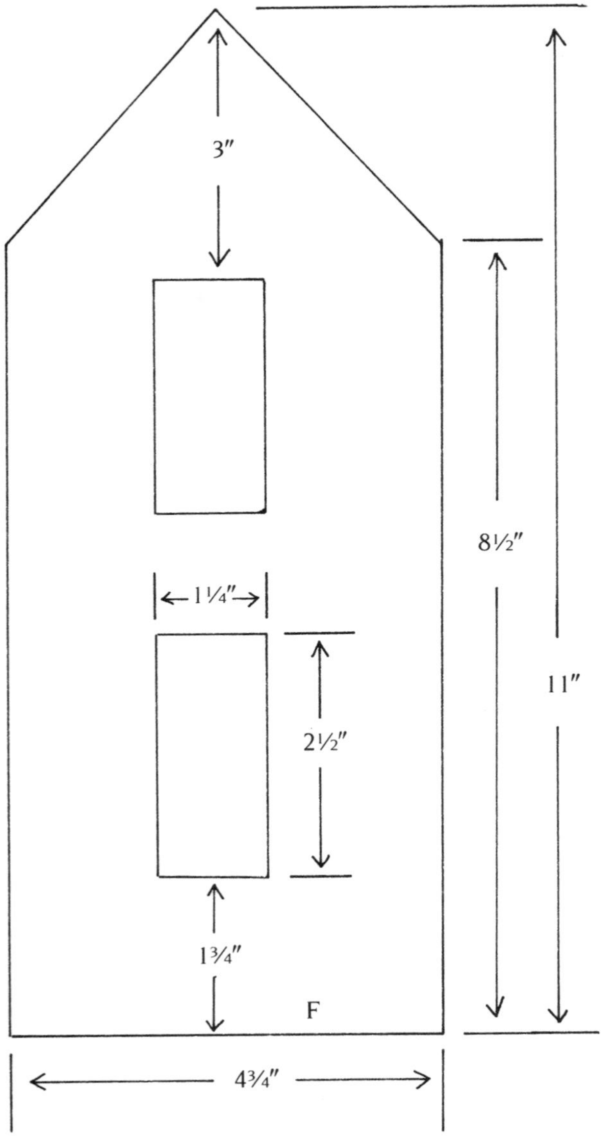

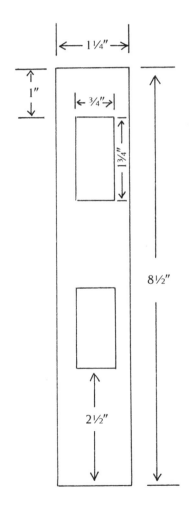

Illus. 82. Wall F

Illus. 83. Turret—cut three.

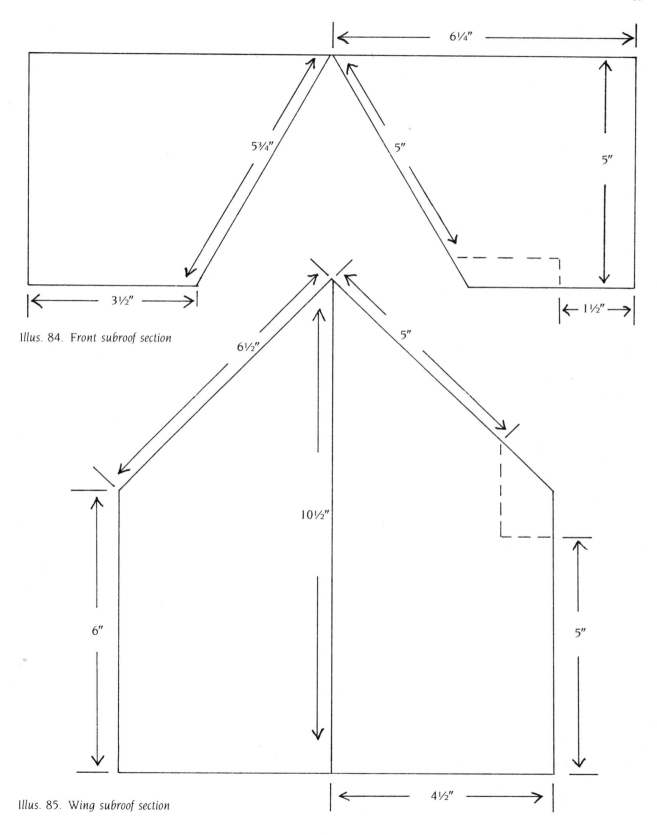

Illus. 84. Front subroof section

Illus. 85. Wing subroof section

64

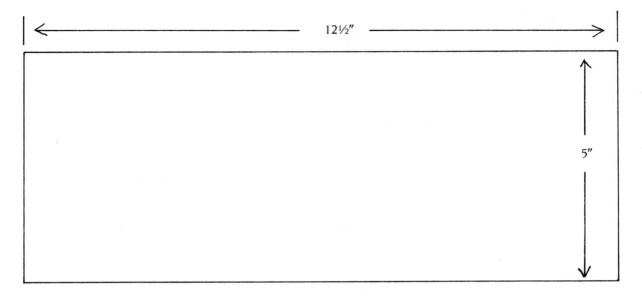

Illus. 86. Back subroof

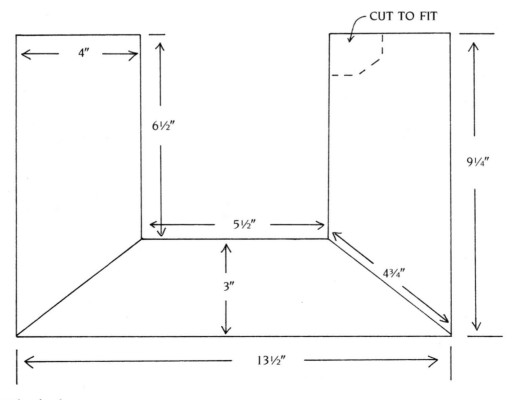

Illus. 87. Porch subroof

Historic Log Cabin.

The Rex, an oldtime movie theatre.

B

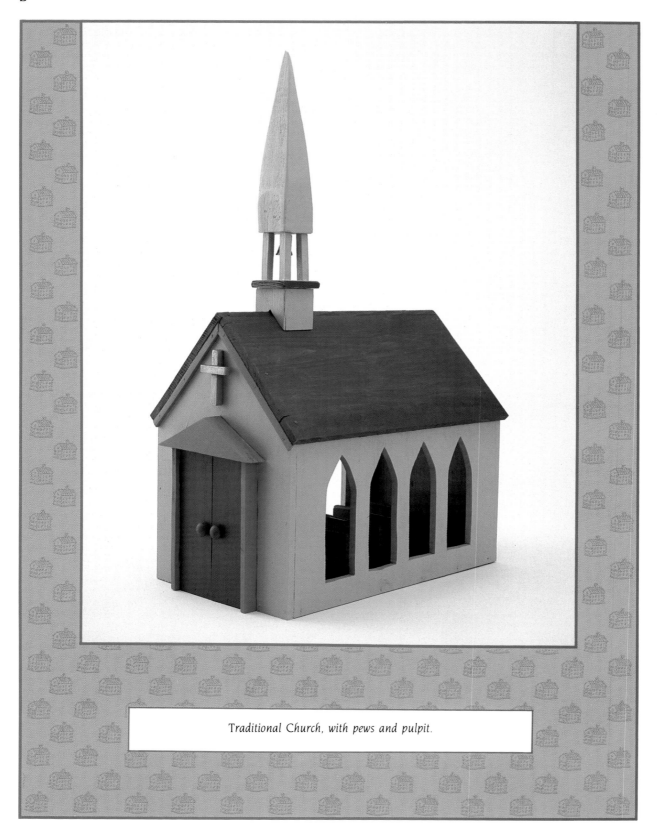

Traditional Church, with pews and pulpit.

C

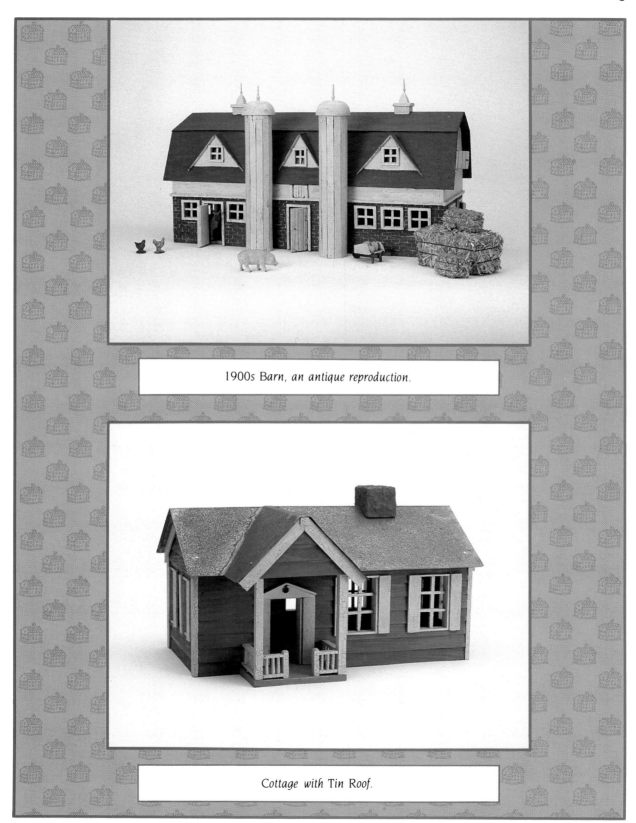

1900s Barn, an antique reproduction.

Cottage with Tin Roof.

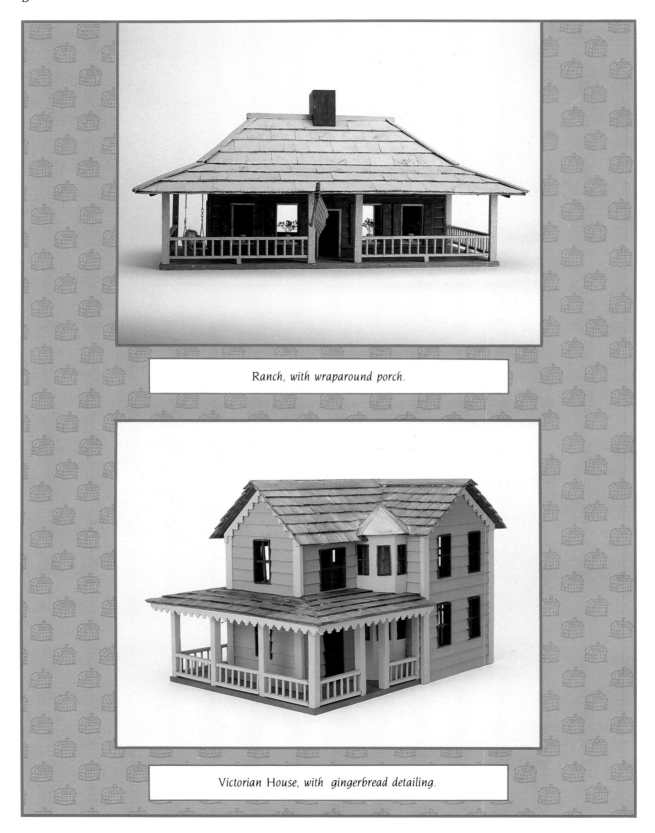

Ranch, with wraparound porch.

Victorian House, with gingerbread detailing.

Two-Storey with Basement.

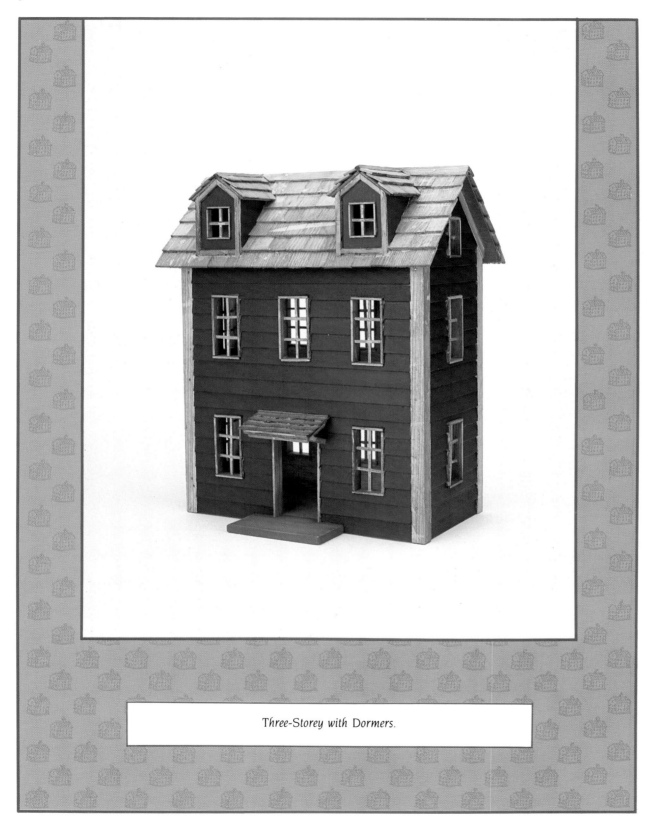

Three-Storey with Dormers.

Farmhouse, with tin roof and chimneys.

Open-front, unfurnished house.

H

House with Picket Fence.

Mission Church.

Block Buildings and Houses.

House Assembly

Cut two ¼″ × ¼″ × 4¾″ pieces, and glue these as spacers between both C sections of the house (Illus. 88). After this has dried thoroughly, glue and nail this and the main house sections together: C to both B sections, and B sections to the largest wall section, A. Refer to Illus. 89 for placement and abutment of these and other sections.

Cut a ¼″ × ¼″ × 6¼″ cross beam, and glue this to the midsections of the top spacer and the top midsection of section A. Illus. 90 shows a plan view of this arrangement.

Connect sections D, E, and F into a wing before attaching them to the other sections. Then glue and nail this wing to the main house, making sure all the corners are square.

Refer to Illus. 89 for the correct position of the turret walls. Sand the inside edges to achieve a mitred fit. Glue them into place.

Cut a roof ridge for the main house sections, ½″ × ½″ × 11¼″. Glue and nail this ridge between both peaks. Then cut a roof ridge for the wing, ½″ × ½″ × 9″. Trim to fit, if necessary, and then glue and nail this piece in place between the roof peak and the other roof ridge (Illus. 91).

Glue and nail the house to the base so that the back of the main house is flush with the base edge as shown in Illus. 89.

Trim

From ½″ wood, cut fourteen feet of strips, ⅛″ × ½″. Cut these strips, to fit, to make window and door trim. Glue these in place so that the inside edges of trim are flush with the inside walls. Also, from ½″ wood, cut six pieces ¼″ × ½″ × 9″ for corner trim. Glue to the front of the B and F sections so that the trim protrudes ¼″ beyond each corner.

Cut one ¼″ × ¼″ × 9″ piece to be used as an inside corner where walls C and E join (Illus. 92). Glue this piece into place.

Siding

From ¾″ wood, cut approximately forty feet of ⅛″ strips for the siding. These may be cut as twenty 24″ pieces, for instance, or forty 12″ pieces.

Illus. 88. Wall C spacers

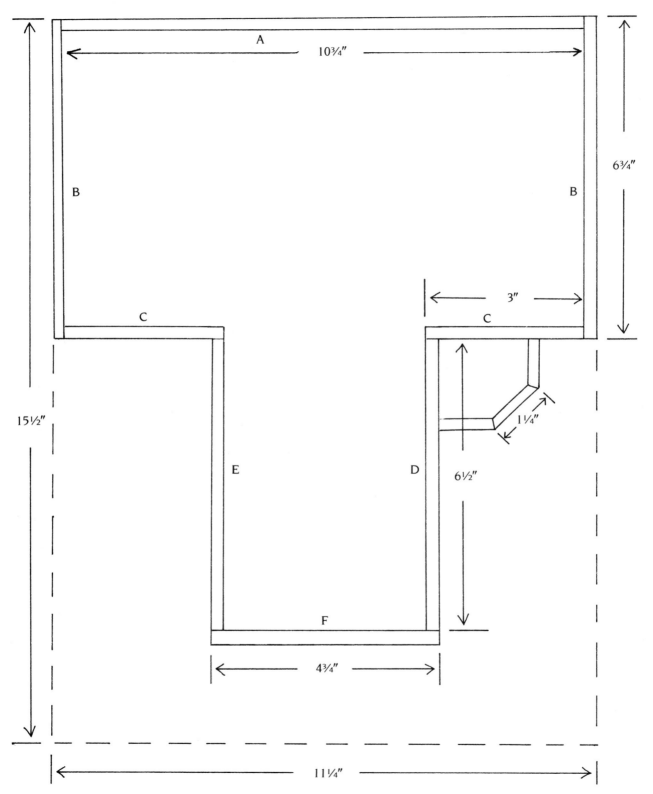

Illus. 89. Top view—house assembly

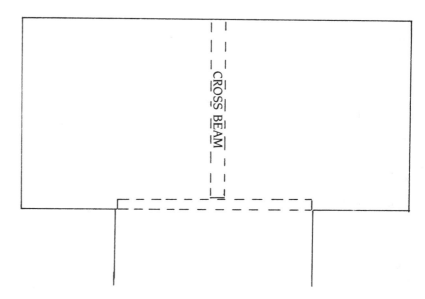

Illus. 90. *Glue the cross beam in place.*

Illus. 91. *After completing the walls, glue and nail the house onto the base.*

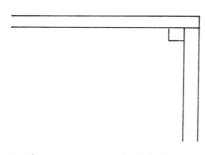

Illus. 92. *Inside corner trim at the C & E joint*

Cut the pieces of siding, to fit, as you progress in applying each row from the bottom to the top. Starting at the bottom, glue the first piece flush with the lowest part of the wall, working on one side at a time. Start the main house siding right at the bottom of the base to completely cover it.

As you work upwards, overlap each row by 1/8" and glue in place. Notch out areas for windows and doors as necessary.

When you have completed applying all of the siding, it is the most suitable time to stain, paint, or wallpaper the inside of the house. Wallpaper is a particularly appropriate choice, since many Victorian homes had not only elaborate stenciling but also used as many as fifteen different wallpapers in one area, walls and ceiling.

Porch Posts, Rafters, and Railings

Using ⅜" wood, cut nine ⅜" × ⅜" × 4" posts. Glue and nail these in place, ⅛" from the porch edge, as you can see in Illus. 76 and in Illus. 93.

Illus. 93. Notch the rafters to fit over the porch supports.

Also from ⅜" wood, cut one ⅜" × ⅜" × 11" roof support and two ⅜" × ⅜" × 8⅜" supports. Glue and nail these on top of the posts.

Make the porch rafters from ¼" × ⅜" strips. You will need a total of 4', so cut: seven 3½" pieces (sides); two 4¼" pieces (corners); and two 2¾" pieces (front).

Notch the rafters to fit over the supports. Sand the end that will join the house to an angle so that the roof will have a slight slope (Illus. 93). Glue and nail the rafters in place, spacing them evenly.

To make the railings, use ¼" wood, and cut four 12" strips ⅛" × ¼". Place two strips together, and tack a brad into each end to hold them securely while you are drilling holes for railing supports.

With a ⅛" bit, drill a hole at each ½" interval. Repeat this procedure for the other set of strips. Cut the strips into sections to fit between the porch posts, leaving room, of course, at doorways.

Now cut thirty-eight (38) 1¼" pieces of the ⅛" diameter dowel. Separate the railings and then apply glue and insert the 1¼" dowel pieces to make railing sections.

Set the railings aside until the house has been painted.

Subroof

Now is the time to cut the notch into the subroof sections that will adjoin the turret. The subroof should fit snug against the turret wall. Glue and nail the main subroof section in place first, and then attach the wing subroof in the same manner.

Also glue and nail the porch subroof into place.

Copper Roof

From the 0.025 gauge copper, cut three pieces according to the dimensions in Illus. 94—one piece marked with bend lines and two triangles. Mark the bend lines, and then using the pliers make a slight bend where indicated. Test the fit of the copper roof pieces before soldering them together. Make any necessary corrections.

Sand the edges to be soldered with a fine emery paper. This will help the solder adhere to the copper.

First join the front section to one back section, soldering from underneath. Then join the remaining piece. Before actually soldering, always make sure the soldering iron is hot to ensure a good joint.

Fasten the copper roof to the subroof with epoxy.

Shingles and Roof Cap

From ¾" wood, cut approximately fifty (50) feet of ⅛" × ¾" strips. Starting with a few strips at a time, cut them into 1" pieces for shingles. Glue a row of shingles to the bottom edge of all of the roof sections, extending over the edge of the subroof by ⅛". Work upwards, overlapping by ⅛" and staggering each row of shingles.

Cut shingles to fit around the turret. When the entire roof is completed, cut, from ⅛" wood, two ⅛" × ¾" × 13" pieces to cap the main roof. Glue and nail these pieces into place.

Then cut two ⅛" × ¾" × 10¾" pieces for the wing roof cap, and glue and nail them into place.

Finishing Touches

To make the window crosspieces use ⅛" × ⅛" strips. You will need a total length of six feet. Cut these to fit each window, and then glue them in place. Use one horizontal piece and two vertical pieces for each window.

As trim typical of a Victorian, use decorative strips 1/16" thick that are premade and available at most craft and hobby shops. Approximately five feet of trim is needed. Cut the trim to fit under all three roof peaks. Glue it into place. Also cut trim for under the porch roof. Fasten these strips to the ends of the rafters with glue and an occasional brad.

Painting

One suggested color combination, which was used here, is to paint the siding a gold ochre color, the window and door trim a dark green, and the turret, corner and decorative trim, and porch posts and railings an off-white. The porch floor is painted brick red.

When everything has dried, the only thing left to do is to glue the railings into place.

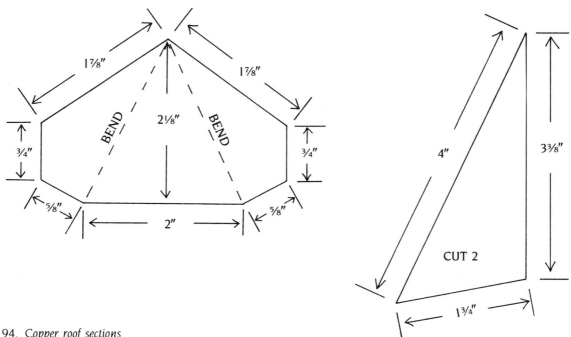

Illus. 94. Copper roof sections

COUNTRY HOUSES

❖ Two-Storey with Basement ❖

Here is an exciting little country house complete with a front and a side porch, both with railings (Illus. 95). Delightful details that add a distinctiveness to this charming but unpretentious house include the front stoop, the side porch steps with lattice work, the double-hung windows, the chimney—and even a faux basement replete with basement windows.

Illus. 95. Two Storey

74

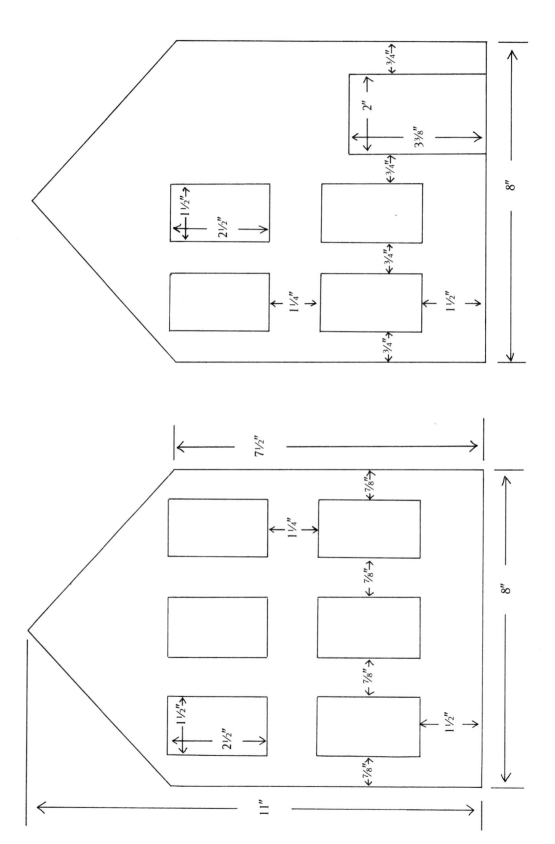

Illus. 97. Right side

Illus. 96. Left side

MATERIALS

Pine, ¼″ thick, 10″ × 6½′
Pine, ⁵⁄₁₆″ thick, 2″ × 20″
Pine, ½″ thick, 6″ × 24″
Pine, ¾″ thick, 10″ × 20″
Luan plywood, ⅛″ thick, 6½″ × 38″
Wood dowels, ⅛″ diameter, 4′
Brads, ⅝″, No. 18, 1 box
Wood glue
Hide glue
Gesso
Sandpaper
Acrylic paint: antique white, dark brown, brick
    red, grey (suggested)
Sand, ¼ cup

TOOLS

Tabletop scroll saw
Band saw
Table saw or radial-arm saw (lattice work—
    optional)
Tack hammer
Drill or drill press (optional)
Drill bits, ⅛″, ½″
Paint brushes

INSTRUCTIONS

Basic Cutting

From the ¼″ pine, first cut the basic house pieces: one base, 8″ × 11¼″; two sides, 8″ × 11″; and two 7½″ × 11¾″ pieces for the front and back. You can follow the dimensions as given in Illus. 96 through Illus. 99. Also cut two 2″ × 8½″ pieces, one 2″ × 11¼″, three 2″ × 3¾″, and two 2″ × 2½″ pieces for the basement foundation.

The porches also may be cut at this time. Follow the dimensions shown in Illus. 100 and Illus. 101.

Cut seven strips from the ½″ wood, ³⁄₁₆″ × 24″, for the window and door frames. Also cut four ¼″ × 7″ strips for the corner trim.

Shingles are cut from the ¾″ wood. Cut sixteen ⅛″ × 20″ strips. Then cut into approximately three hundred (300) one-inch pieces for the individual shingles. Cut twenty-four more ⅛″ × 20″ strips to be used for siding.

Also cut two 6½″ × 13¼″ pieces from ⅛″ plywood for the subroof at this time.

You may also want to cut a chimney piece from ¾″ pine; or you can wait until the structure is essentially complete and then adjust the dimensions to match the final touch you want for your house.

Windows and Doors

Draw the window and door openings as depicted in Illus. 96 through Illus. 99. All of the window openings are the same, 1½″ wide by 2½″ high.

First cut out the doors. Then, drill a ½″ hole into the middle of the area where each window will be cut out. Detach the blade from the scroll saw, and insert it through one of the holes. Reattach the blade, and then carefully cut out the window. Repeat this procedure for each window.

House Assembly

First glue and nail the sides to the base. Then glue and nail the front and back into place.

From ¾″ pine, cut a ¾″ × 11¼″ strip for the roof ridge. Glue and nail this into place between the roof peaks.

Window, Door, and Corner Trim

From the seven previously cut strips, ½″ × ³⁄₁₆″ × 24″, carefully cut and fit pieces to frame each window and door.

Glue this framing in place so that the inside edges of the trim are flush with the inside walls. The trim pieces will protrude ¼″ so that the siding will have room to meet flush against the framing.

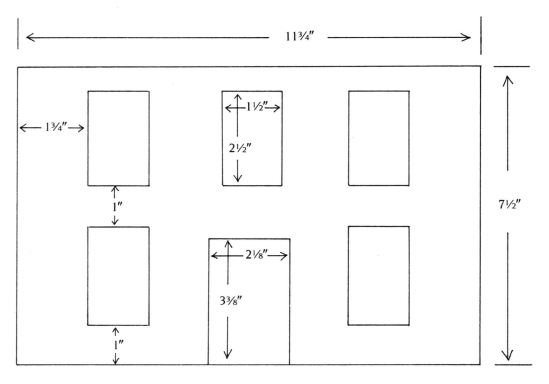

Illus. 98. Front

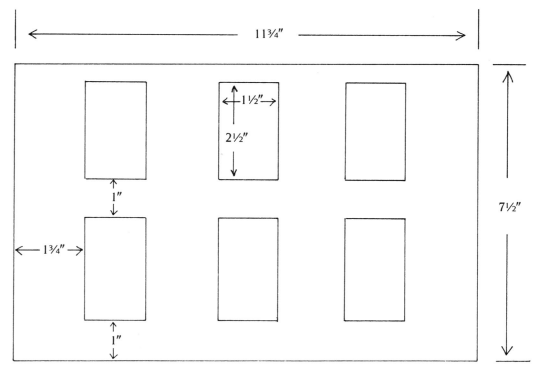

Illus. 99. Back

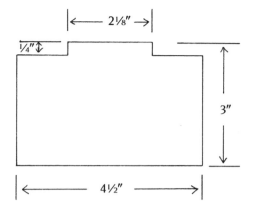

Illus. 100. Front porch floor

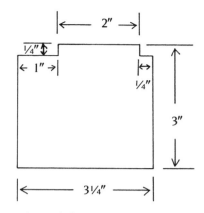

Illus. 101. Side porch floor

Cut each corner trim piece and sand the edges to correspond with the pitch of the roof. Glue and nail the four 7″ corner trim pieces onto front and back corners, with each trim piece extending ¼″ beyond the side.

Siding

Using the twenty-four previously cut strips, ⅛″ × ¾″ × 20″, cut and fit siding for one side at a time. Start from the bottom (overlapping the base), and glue on the first piece.

Each subsequent piece should overlap the previous piece. Glue each piece in place working upwards. Cut to fit around windows and doors, notching the piece of siding when necessary.

Roof

Determine the proper placement of the subroof sections. The subroof will extend about ½″ all of the way around. Then glue and nail sections into place.

If the shingles have not been cut yet, here is a reminder that it's time to cut the sixteen (16) strips from ¾″ wood that measure ⅛″ × 20″. And as stated before, you then need to cut about three hundred (300) one-inch pieces for the individual shingles.

Start from the bottom roof edge and work up. The bottom row of shingles should extend ⅛″ both below the bottom edge and just be-

yond the side edges of the subroof. Glue the first row in place, and overlap each successive row ¼″ on top of the previous row.

Make the roof cap by cutting two ⅛″ × 13½″ strips from ¾″ thick pine. Glue these in place to finish the top of the roof as can be seen in Illus. 95.

Cut four pieces, ⅛″ × ¼″ × 6¼″, for the peak trim. Cut or sand the ends to fit under the eaves.

Foundation

Assemble your 2″-wide foundation pieces. You should have eight pieces cut. Follow Illus. 102 to determine the placement of the basement windows. All the basement windows are 2″ wide and only 1″ high (Illus. 103). Cut out the windows.

Glue and nail the foundation together according to the layout of Illus. 102. Be careful to check that all the corners are square.

Apply a thin bead of wood glue to the top of the foundation, and then carefully arrange the house on top of it, overlapping the foundation as shown in Illus. 103. Make sure that the front door is above the porch section.

Porches

From ¼″-thick pine, now you will need to cut flooring for the porches, if not already done with the other items covered under Basic Cut-

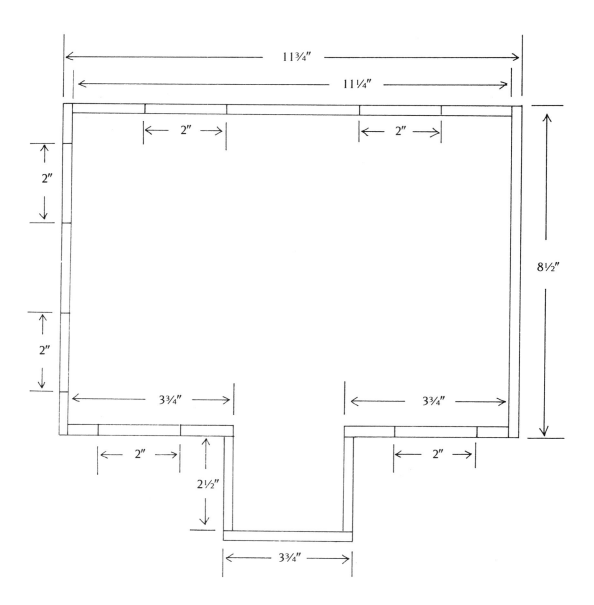

Illus. 102. *Foundation*

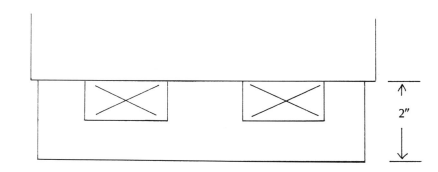

Illus. 103. *Side view, house on
foundation*

ting. Refer to Illus. 100 and Illus. 101 if you still need to cut these pieces.

For the side porch foundation cut a ¼″ × 2″ × 8″ piece of latticed wood. As an option you can use a piece of prelatticed wood.

To cut the lattice, turn and lock the saw blade at a 45° angle. Using ¼″ wood, make ⅛″-deep cuts. Pull the saw across the wood two times to cut a ¼″-wide gouge. Continue similar cuts every ¼″.

Turn the strip over, and repeat the process at this same angle and depth. This will leave a crisscross pattern.

From the lattice or solid wood, cut two 2″ × 2¼″ pieces and one 2″ × 2½″ piece. Also cut two 5⁄16″ × 5⁄16″ × 2″ pieces for support posts.

Glue the foundation to the right side of the house, to correspond with the porch flooring, following the diagram in Illus. 104.

Glue and nail both pieces of porch flooring in place.

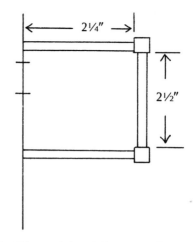

Illus. 104. Side porch foundation—top view

Steps

The dimensions of the stringers for each set of steps are given in Illus. 105 and Illus. 106. Cut two each from ¼″ pine.

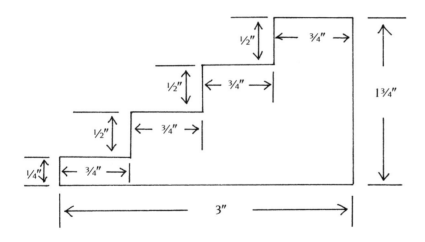

Illus. 105. Stringer, front steps

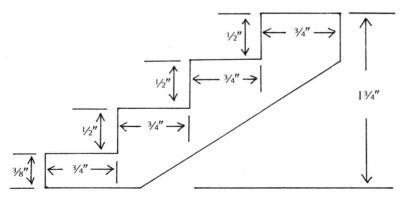

Illus. 106. Stringer, side steps

For the front porch, from ⅛" plywood, cut four steps, ⅛" × ¾" × 4½", and four risers, ⅛" × ½" × 3¾".

For the side porch, also from ⅛" plywood, cut four steps, ⅛" × ¾" × 2½", and four risers, ⅛" × ½" × 2¼".

Glue the supports in place; next glue the risers and then the steps (Illus. 107).

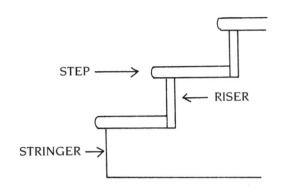

Illus. 107. Steps, side view

Handrails and Posts

Using the 5/16" pine, cut four posts, 5/16" × 5/16" × 1½", for the porches themselves, then cut three posts, 5/16" × 5/16" × 2⅛", for the bottom steps.

Also from 5/16" wood, cut two ⅛" × 20" strips to be used for the upper and lower handrails. Place these strips together, and tack a brad into each end to hold securely while holes are drilled for dowels.

With a ⅛" bit, drill a hole at each ¼" interval (Illus. 108). Then cut three 2" sections, one 2½" section, and three 3" sections. Separate the handrails. Then cut the ⅛"-diameter dowel into 1¼" lengths.

Glue and insert the 1¼"-long dowel pieces into the 2" sections and 2½" section, which will be used for the porch railings (Illus. 109).

In order to insert the dowels at an angle for the step rails (the 3" sections), hold a double section at an angle to the drill bit to angle

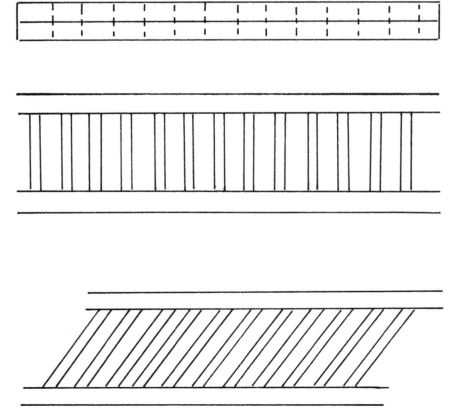

Illus. 108. Handrail assembly

Window Crosspieces

Cut four strips from ¼" pine, ⅛" × 10". From these cut six 1" lengths, and twenty-one (21) 1⅜" lengths.

Sand to fit, and then glue, horizontally, one of the 1⅜" pieces into each opening of the large windows of the house proper.

Glue one of the 1" pieces vertically into each basement foundation window. All of the pieces should be positioned carefully in the middle of the window opening.

As a finishing touch, cut from the remaining siding strips to trim around the front door and above the side door.

Painting

One suggested color combination for paint, used here, is to select dark brown for the siding and antique white for the window and door trim and porch railings. Shingles can be given a grey wash (diluted). You can paint the porches and steps with brick red, and then mix some sand with red for the chimney and basement finish. This may be patted on with your finger or an old brush.

Illus. 109. Railings

slightly the previously drilled holes. Repeat this procedure with each hole. If you have a drill press, it will simplify this step.

Glue and insert the dowel pieces to complete the step rails.

Glue the posts as shown in Illus. 110. Add the completed railings as shown in Illus. 95.

Illus. 110. Glue the porch posts in place.

Three-Storey House
❖ with Dormers ❖

This quaint country house, complete with dormer windows, is sure to be a favorite. Stained trim adds a rustic touch (Illus. 111).

Illus. 111. Three-Storey House

MATERIALS

Pine, or plywood, ¼" thick, 12" × 4'
Pine, ½" thick, 6" × 12" (cut fourteen pieces, ⅜" × ½" × 12", for windows)

Pine, ¾" thick, 6" × 24" (cut twenty-two pieces, ⅜" × ¾" × 24", for siding)
Plywood or panelling, ⅛" thick, 10" × 18" (sub-roof)
Corner molding, ½" × ½" × 4'
Wood, 1/16" thick, ¼" × 16" (peak trim), ⅛" × 18" (dormer trim)
Pine, ¾" thick, 1" × 9½" (roof support)

Note: Thin strips, as required, for window trim and crosspieces can be purchased ready-cut at hobby and craft shops or shops that sell materials for making dollhouses and miniatures. Also available are precut shingles.

Wood, ⅛" × ⅛" × 10' (cut to fit for window crosspieces)
Wood, ¼" × ¼" × 12" (for roof dormer supports, dormer caps)
Roof: You will need cedar shakes to cover an area of approximately 10" × 12" or pine shingles made from ⅛" × ¾" strips (optional: you can substitute tin roof for subroof and shingles)
Brads, ¾", No. 18, one box
Wood glue
Hide glue
Gesso
Sandpaper
Stain, light color
Acrylic paint: dark green and brick red (suggested)

TOOLS

Tabletop scroll saw
Band saw
Table saw
Tack hammer
Block plane (optional)
Drill
Drill bit, ½″
Paint brushes

INSTRUCTIONS

Basic Cutting

Following the dimensions given in Illus. 112, Illus. 113, and Illus. 114, cut the ¼″ wood for the front, back, two sides, and porch.

For the window and door trim, cut the ½″ wood into fourteen (14) strips, ⅜″ × ½″ × 12″.

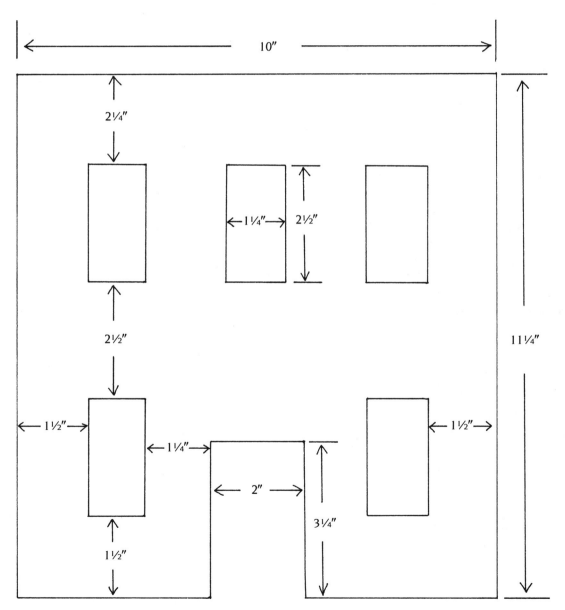

Illus. 112. Front—use the same dimensions for the back but without the door and with an extra window.

Then, from the ¾" wood, cut twenty-two (22) pieces, ⅜" × ¾" × 24", to be used for the siding.

From the corner moulding, cut four 11" pieces.

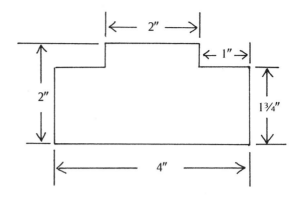

Illus. 114. Porch

Windows

Draw the windows and door in place on all the main house sections. Then, using a ½" drill bit, drill a hole into the middle of the area outlined for each window.

Disconnect the blade to the tabletop scroll, then saw and slide the blade through one of the holes. Reattach the blade, and then carefully cut out the window. Repeat this procedure for each required opening.

House Assembly

Spread a thin bead of glue on the side edges of both side sections. Glue the house together so that the sides are inset into the front and back sections. Then nail the joints together using several brads for each corner.

Once the glue has set, place the house on the remaining piece of ¼" wood, leaving an adequate piece from which to cut the dormers. Pencil along the *inside* perimeter of the house, and then cut out this section for the house floor, cutting just along the outside of your pencil line. Glue and nail the floor into place. Also glue and nail the porch floor.

Stain or paint the inside of the house at this point.

Roof Support

Cut a roof support from ¾" wood. The finished piece should measure ¾" × 1" × 9½", but

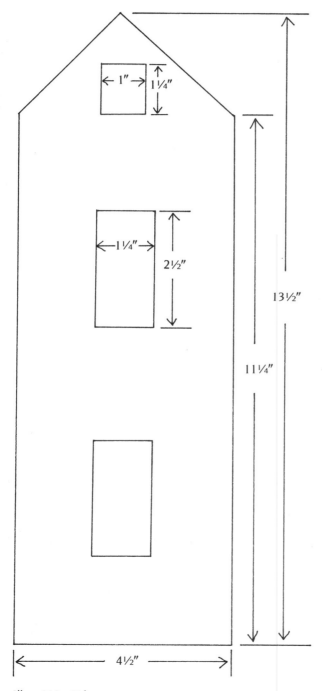

Illus. 113. Side

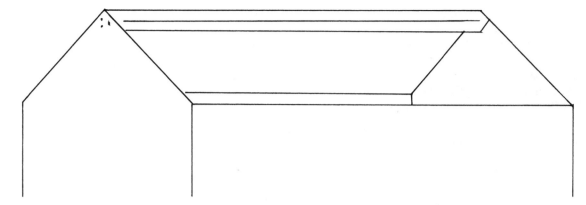

Illus. 115. *Glue and nail the roof support between the peaks.*

carefully measure the inside distance between the roof peaks before cutting.

Using either a band saw or a block plane, trim away the top edges of the support so that the shape coincides with the slope of the rooftop. Glue and nail the support into place (Illus. 115).

Attach the 11" lengths of corner trim as shown in Illus. 111. These should be glued and nailed into place.

Window Frames

Cut, to fit, four pieces for each window frame from the ⅜" × ½" × 12" strips. When you are gluing the frames, be sure the inside edge of the pieces are flush with the inside walls. Glue the frames only, since the siding remains to be added. Also attach the door frame in the same manner.

Siding

Starting from the bottom, measure and cut, to fit, pieces of siding from the previously cut strips. As you work upwards, overlap each row by ⅛". Glue the strips of siding into place.

Peak Trim

Cut four pieces of peak trim to fit along the roof line (Illus. 116). These can be cut from remaining window strips; cut two of the strips in half lengthwise using the band saw.

Then cut, to fit, two pieces for each peak. To shape the peak ends for the correct mitred fit, hold each piece at the appropriate angle against a sanding wheel (Illus. 117). Glue into place.

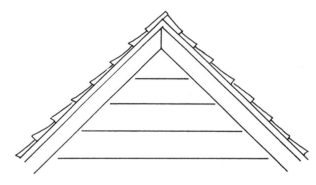

Illus. 116. *Peak trim*

Illus. 117. *Sand one end of the peak trim pieces for a mitred fit.*

Roof and Subroof

If you are going to use pine shingles, then you will need a subroof. Cut two 4½″ × 11¼″ pieces of the ⅛″ wood for the subroof; then glue and nail these in place.

If you are going to have a tin roof rather than the shingles, then there will be no need for the subroof. In that case, attach the dormers directly to the tin roof.

Dormers

From the ¼″ wood, cut four triangular dormer sides to the dimensions given in Illus. 118. Then cut two dormer fronts from the ¼″ wood, using the dimensions in Illus. 119. From ⅛″ wood, also cut four roof sections following the dimensions in Illus. 120.

Using the ½″ bit, drill a hole into the space to be cut for the window for each dormer front. Disconnect the blade to the scroll saw, and slide the blade through one of the holes. Re-attach the blade, and then carefully cut out the window. Repeat this procedure for the second window.

Glue the fronts to the sides of the dormers. When dry, sand the bottom edges of the dormer to fit flush with the subroof (or tin roof). Dormer fronts should be parallel to the house front. Cut and glue window trim to fit, and then glue the dormer roof sections in place (sanding as necessary for a flush fit).

A delightful detail, which is purely optional, is to cut thin ⅛″ strips from the remaining siding strips to trim the entire dormer front.

Shingles

If you are using pine shingles, cut ⅛″ × ¾″ strips into 1″ pieces. Starting from the bottom of the roofline, glue shingles in place one row at a time, horizontally. Overlap the next row of shingles by ¼″, continuing upwards with over-lapping shingles staggered by about half the width of a shingle. Shingle the dormer roofs in the same way.

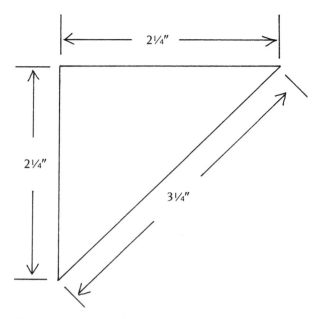

Illus. 118. Dormer side

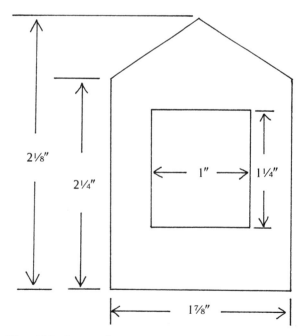

Illus. 119. Dormer front

Roof Caps

Cut two 11½″ pieces from the remaining siding strips. Cap the roof with these, cutting to fit around the dormers. Glue and nail the pieces in place.

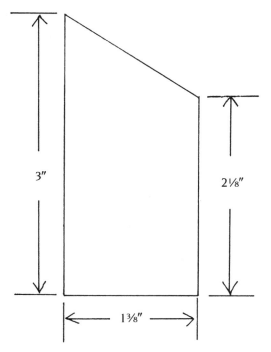

3"

2⅛"

1⅜"

Illus. 120. Dormer roof

From the ¼" × ¼" piece, cut two 3⅜" pieces for the dormer roof caps. Sand these to fit, and then glue them in place.

Porch Roof

From the ⅛" wood, cut a subroof 1½" × 2¾". Then cut, from the ¼" × ¼" wood, two 1¼" supports.

Glue the subroof, at a slant, approximately one inch above the door frame. Sand and then glue the roof supports in place as shown in Illus. 121.

When these are dry, add shingles to the porch roof in the same manner as for the main roof.

Window Crosspieces

The window crosspieces are a completely optional feature. But, if you decide to include them, you won't be disappointed by the distinctive charm they bring.

If you have not purchased precut strips for the crosspieces, cut ten feet of ⅛" × ⅛" strips.

Measure and cut pieces to fit each window individually, as your windows may vary slightly. Glue the horizontal crosspieces in place first, then the vertical pieces.

Even though this procedure is time consuming, it is just this sort of detail that can add the right finishing touch to the overall look of a house.

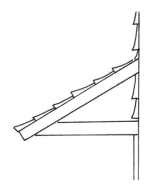

Illus. 121. Porch roof, side view

Painting

As a suggestion that was used here, select a dark green color for siding and a brick red color for the porch floor (Illus. 122). Stain all the remaining areas with a light-color stain.

Illus. 122. Paint with dark green acrylic paint.

❖ Cottage with Tin Roof ❖

This little vacation cottage features a tin roof and an old-timey front porch (Illus. 123). Try a version without siding for a simpler, more pared-down country look.

Illus. 123. Cottage with Tin Roof

MATERIALS

Pine, ¼" thick, 3½ board feet

Pine, ½" thick, 8" × 12" (cut ten (10) ⅛" × ½" × 12" pieces for shutters, window, and door frames)

Pine, ¾" thick, 8" × 12"
(cut eighteen (18) ¾" × ⅛" × 12" pieces for siding;
cut one (1) ¾" × ¾" × 12" piece for roof ridge; and
cut one (1) ¾" × ¼" × 5½" piece for porch ridge)

Wood, 1½" thick, 1½" × 1½" (chimney)

Tin (or flashing), 10" × 20"

Solder

Brads, ¾", No. 18, one box

Wood glue

Hide glue

Gesso

Sandpaper

Stain, medium color

Acrylic paint: grey-blue, antique white, brick red (suggested)

TOOLS

Tabletop scroll saw
Band saw
Table saw
Tack hammer
Drill
Drill bit, ½"
Soldering iron
Paint brushes
Tin snips

INSTRUCTIONS

Basic Cutting

Following the dimensions given in Illus. 124, Illus. 125, and Illus. 126, cut the ¼" wood for the front, back, and the two sides. Also cut four ¼" × ⅜" × 5" strips for the corner trim. The base piece should be cut to roughly 5½" × 12"; however, be sure to measure the actual

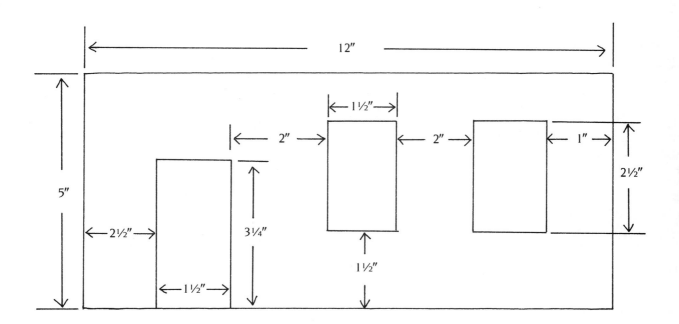

Illus. 124. Dimensions

dimensions of your main structure pieces before you cut the base, to ensure an accurate fit.

Cut the ½″ wood into ten (10) strips, ⅛″ × ½″ × 12″, to be used for the shutter, window, and door frames. Cut two additional strips, ¼″ × ½″ × 12″. Then cut these into four pieces, 3¼″ long, for the rafters.

From the ¾″ wood, cut eighteen (18) strips, ¾″ × ⅛″ × 12″, to be used for the siding. Then cut a ¾″ × ¾″ × 12″ piece for the roof ridge

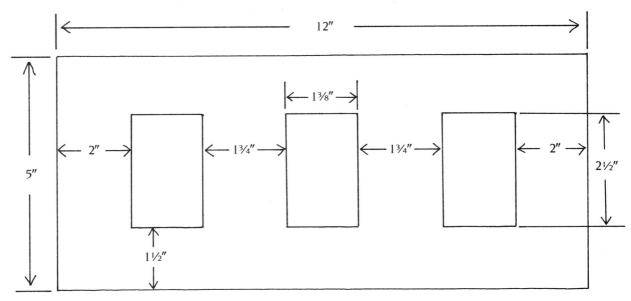

Illus. 125. Dimensions

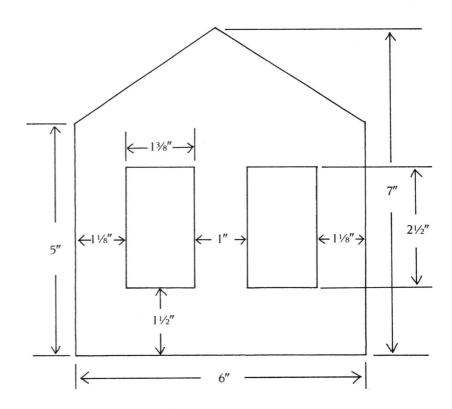

Illus. 126. Dimensions

and a ¾″ × ¼″ × 5½″ piece for the porch ridge.

Windows and Door

Again following the dimensions in Illus. 124, Illus. 125, and Illus. 126, draw the corresponding windows and door in place on all main house sections. Using the ½″ drill bit, drill a hole into the middle of the area outlined for each window.

Disconnect the blade of the tabletop scroll saw, and slide the blade through one of the holes. Reattach the blade, and then carefully cut out the window. Repeat this procedure for each of the windows, and then cut out the door opening.

House Assembly

Spread a thin layer of glue on all the edges of the base piece. Use the ¾″ brads to nail the front and back to the base. Next, spread a thin bead of glue on the side edges of both the front and back sections, and then attach the sides (Illus. 127). Nail the joints together using several brads for each corner.

Fit the ¾″ × ¾″ × 12″ piece for the roof ridge between the peaks. Glue and nail the roof ridge piece in place.

Once you've finished this stage, you are ready to stain or paint the inside of the house.

Corner Trim

Attach the 5″ lengths of corner trim to the front and back corners as shown in Illus. 127. The trim should extend beyond the side by ³⁄₁₆″. Glue and nail each corner trim piece in place.

Window and Door Frames, Siding

Cut, to fit, four pieces for each window frame from the ⅛″ × ½″ × 12″ strips, and cut three pieces for the door frame from the same strips. Glue the frames into place so that their inside edges are flush with the inside walls. You may also want to add window crosspieces at this point, similar to those shown in Illus. 123.

Working from the bottom, measure and cut to fit, pieces of siding from previously cut ⅛″ × ¾″ strips. As you work upwards, overlap each row by ⅛″. Glue each row into place as you go.

Porch

Using the dimensions given in Illus. 128, cut the porch base from ¼″ wood. Glue this piece into place.

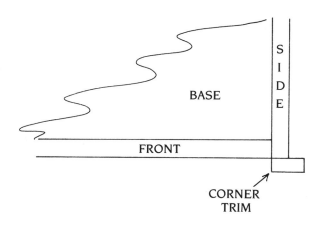

Illus. 127. *Top view of wall construction*

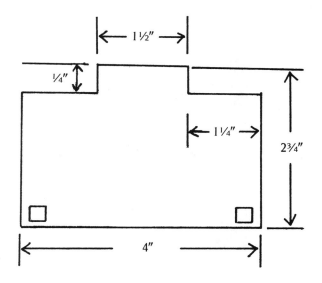

Illus. 128. *Porch base*

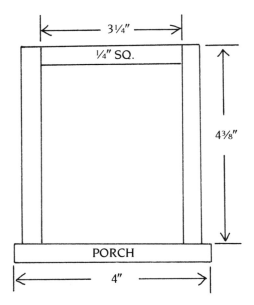

Illus. 129. Front view, porch posts and supports

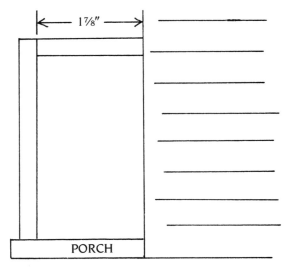

Illus. 130. Side view, porch posts

Also from the ¼″ wood, cut two porch posts, ¼″ × 4⅜″, and the roof supports: two, ¼″ × 1⅞″; and one, ¼″ × 3¼″. Follow Illus. 129 and Illus. 130 to assemble the posts and roof support. Glue and nail them into place.

Rafters and Porch Ridge

Cut a notch in one end of the porch ridge to make a flush fitting with the main roof ridge (Illus. 131). Notch the rafters, as shown in Illus. 132, where they will rest on the cross beams of the porch.

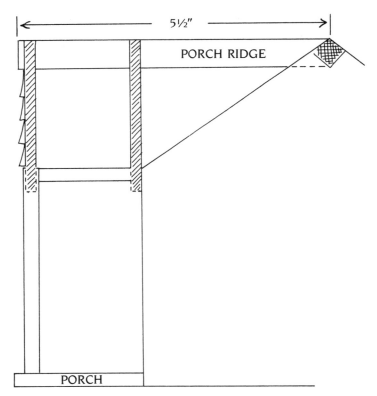

Illus. 131. Side view, porch ridge/rafters

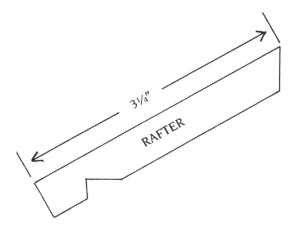

Illus. 132. *Notch rafters*

Glue the rafters and porch ridge in place. Basically this will be one step, because they will be supporting each other (Illus. 133).

Put siding on the front of the porch peak.

Shutters

From the remaining ½" × ⅛" strips, cut two shutters for each window, the length of the windows. Also cut two pieces the length of the door, plus a triangular trim piece for above the door. You can give the triangular trim piece a slight Greek revival flair by drilling a hole just below the crest, as can be seen in Illus. 123. Paint the shutters before gluing them to the house.

Painting

An option that you can consider for this charming cottage is to give the house an old crackled look. First paint the entire cottage with a thin layer of hide glue. Let this dry for four hours.

Illus. 133. *Porch ridge without the tin roof*

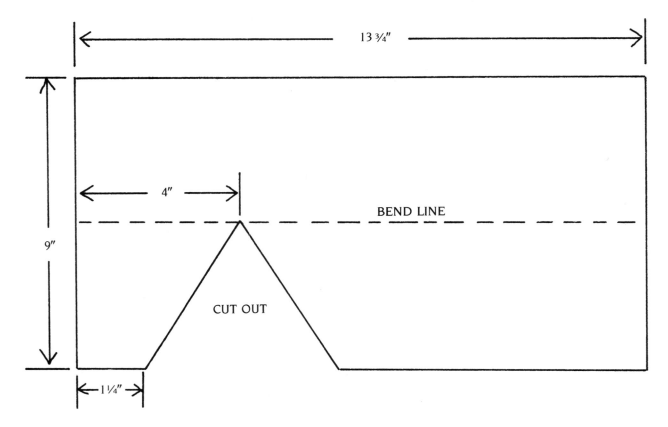

Illus. 134. *Main roof dimensions*

Mix acrylic paint with gesso (2 tablespoons gesso to 1 tablespoon paint). The more gesso you use the smaller the cracks will be.

A suggestion is to paint the house a grey-blue with antique white trim. Paint the chimney and porch floor a brick red color.

When the paint has completely dried, glue the shutters in place.

Roof

Using the dimensions given in Illus. 134 and Illus. 135, cut both of the tin roof sections with tin snips, and then make the appropriate bends to fit the roof ridges. Tack on the large roof section at all four corners. Position the porch roof so that the seams are flush with the main roof, then solder them together (Illus. 136). Tack the front porch roof corners to the supports.

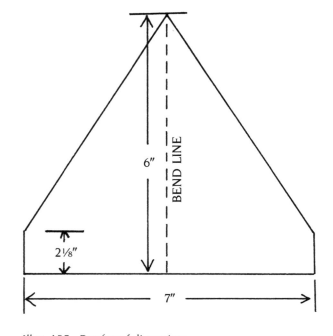

Illus. 135. *Porch roof dimensions*

Illus. 136. Soldering the tin roof

Chimney

From the 1½″ × 1½″ piece previously cut for the chimney, cut out a "V" to match the roof slope for a proper fit. Using wood glue, attach the chimney to the tin roof.

Porch Railing

Another optional detail that you may enjoy adding is the railings for the front porch. To make the porch railings, follow the instructions for making "Handrails and Posts" in the Two-Storey House with Basement project (page 80). Of course, adjust the dimensions for the handrails to fit the Cottage porch, but the basic steps are all the same.

❖ House with Picket Fence ❖

This is a basic little house that sits on a base surrounded by a white picket fence and a green lawn (Illus. 137). Some delightful touches to this simple but quaint country house are the hinged front and back doors, a "gate" for the picket fence, and decorative trim and an attic window for each gable.

MATERIALS

Wood, ¾" thick, 16" × 16"
Wood, ¼" thick, 10" × 6½'
Wood trim, ¼" square, 8'
Wood trim, ⅛" dental moulding, 2'
Wood, 1" × 1" square, 2¾" length

Illus. 137. House with Picket Fence

Wood glue
Brads, ¾", No. 18, one box
Hinges, ¾" brass; four
Flat wood plug, ⅜"; one

Tin, 9" × 16"
Acrylic paint: off white, dark green, grey, brick
    red, thalo bronze
    (suggested)

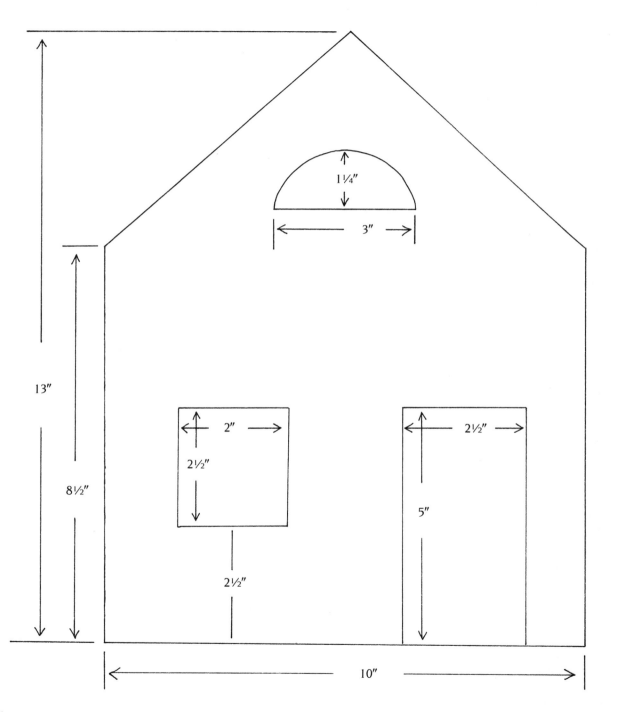

Illus. 138. Front—(use the same dimensions for the back)

TOOLS

Table, radial-arm, or band saw
Tabletop scroll saw
Drill, with ½" bit, ¹⁄₁₆" bit
Tack hammer
Jeweler's screwdriver
Tin snips

INSTRUCTIONS

Basic Cutting

From ¼" wood, cut out the front, back, and the two sides according to the dimensions given in Illus. 138 and Illus. 139. Also cut out two doors, 2½" × 5", from this wood.

Cut a base for the fence from ¾" wood measuring 16" × 16".

Windows and Doors

Draw the door and window openings on the house pieces. Then, drill a ½" hole into the middle of the area drawn for each window opening (Illus. 140). Cut out the openings with the tabletop scroll saw.

To do this, first detach the blade, and then insert the blade through one of the holes. Reattach the blade, and cut out the window area. Repeat this procedure for each window and door.

House Assembly

Glue and nail the sides to the front and back sections (Illus. 141). Then set the structure on a piece of ¼" wood, and draw a line around the inside perimeter to mark the base piece. Cut this piece out, and then glue and nail it into place.

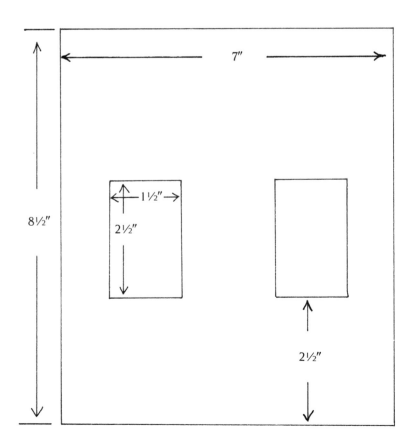

Illus. 139. Side

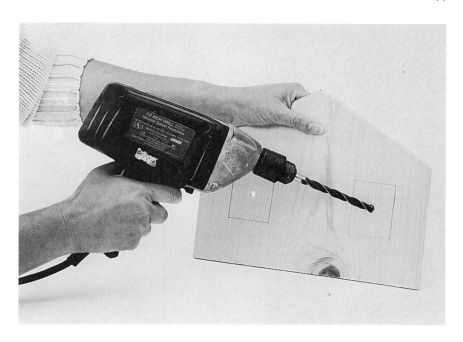

Illus. 140. Drill a hole into each window area.

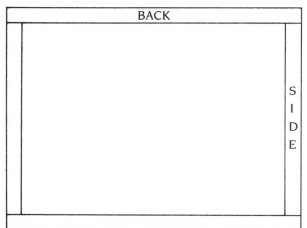

Illus. 141. Glue and nail the sides to the back and front.

Sand the doors to fit, and then attach them to the house with two hinges each. A small jeweler's screwdriver is needed for this task.

Stain or paint the inside of the house at this point.

Fence

To complete the fence, cut sixteen (16) strips of ¼" wood, ½" × 15". Keep four this length, and then cut forty-eight (48) 3½" lengths for the pickets from the remaining twelve strips. Taper these small pieces to a point at one end as shown in Illus. 142.

Glue together four sections of fence using twelve 3½" pieces and one 15" piece for each section. Glue the long crosspiece approximately one inch from the top of the picket points. Let these dry thoroughly, and then glue a section to each side of the 16" × 16" base.

Cut a ¼" strip to glue diagonally across three pickets to look like a gate (Illus. 137).

Roof

Using tin snips, cut a 9" × 16" piece of tin for the roof. Bend this piece in half parallel to the short dimension. This can be accomplished by setting the roof halfway on and halfway off a table or work bench with a sharp, 90° edge, and then pushing down on the unsupported half (close to the bend). Bend the piece partway, and then check for fit.

After you have reached the proper angle for the bend, set the roof on the house. Position it with an equal distance of overhang in the front and the back. From underneath draw a line on the tin against the front and back overhang.

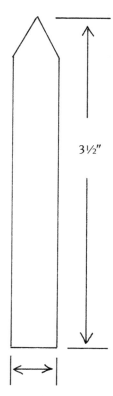

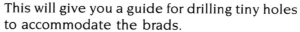

Illus. 142. *Pickets for fence*

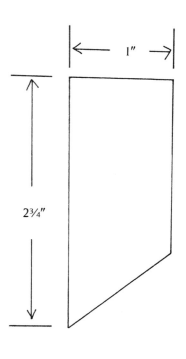

Illus. 143. *Chimney*

This will give you a guide for drilling tiny holes to accommodate the brads.

Drill several holes ($\frac{1}{16}$" bit) along each line, but about $\frac{1}{8}$" in from the line. It is extremely important to check the alignment with the wood before drilling the holes.

Nail the roof in place. Then cut a chimney from 1" × 1" wood, 2¾" long. Cut one corner off to fit the angle of the roof (Illus. 143).

Trim

From the ¼" dental moulding, cut, to fit, trim pieces for along the front roofline and across the front as shown in Illus. 137.

Use the ¼" × ¼" pieces to trim around the windows and door frames. Also cut cross-pieces for the windows and dividers for the arched windows. Cut two front shutters from ¼" wood, ¾" × 2½". Glue the trim pieces in place.

Painting

Use an off-white color to paint the picket fence and the trim work. A suggested combination is to paint the house grey, the roof a dark green, and the yard a watered-down green.

The house may be glued to the yard, or it can remain freestanding.

HOUSES OF WORSHIP

❖ Traditional Church ❖

This little country church is a unique but classic shape (Illus. 144). Featured are a bell tower, high, arched windows, and an interior complete with pews and pulpit.

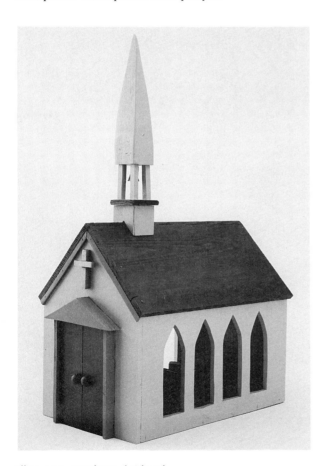

Illus. 144. Traditional Church

MATERIALS

Wood, ¼" thick, 8" × 8'
Wood, ½" thick, 6" × 6"
Wood, ¾" thick, 2" × 3"
Wood, 1½" × 1½", 9" length
Wood glue
Brads, ¾", No. 18, one box
Brass bell, ¾"; one
Wood button plugs, ⅜", two (doorknobs)
Acrylic paint: ivory, brick, thalo bronze (suggested)
Stain, medium color

TOOLS

Table, radial-arm, or band saw
Tabletop scroll saw
Drill with ½" bit
Tack hammer
Needlenose pliers

INSTRUCTIONS

Basic Cutting

Cut out the two sides, the front, and the back from ¼" wood following the dimensions in Illus. 145 and Illus. 146. Also cut out the two 2" × 5¼" doors at this time.

Windows

Draw four windows on both of the side pieces. These windows are positioned 1″ from the bottom and 1″ apart. Use the dimensions in Illus. 146.

Drill a ½″ hole into each window area, then, using the scroll saw, cut out each window. To do this, detach the blade and insert it into one of the holes, then reattach the blade. Make preliminary cuts to the corners (backing up to the middle after each cut) for ease in cutting out the windows.

Church Construction

Glue and nail the front and back to the sides. Then set the structure on a piece of ¼″ wood. Trace the inside perimeter with a pencil. Cut out this base piece by keeping the saw blade just on the outside of the pencil line. Then glue and nail the base in place.

Pews and Pulpit

From ¼″ wood, cut five pews: five 1½″ × 4″ pieces, and five ½″ × 4″ pieces (Illus. 147).

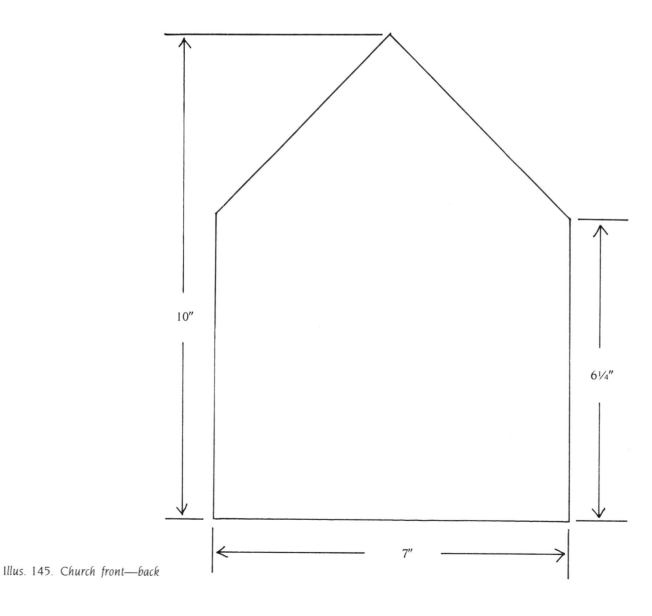

10″

6¼″

7″

Illus. 145. Church front—back

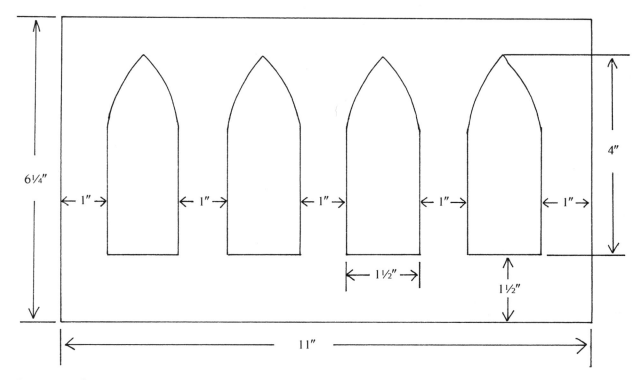

Illus. 146. Side

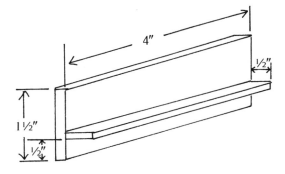

Illus. 147. Pew

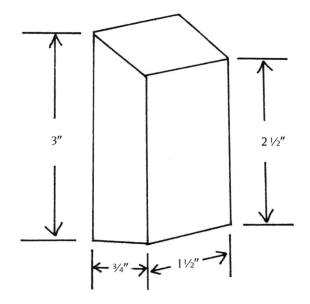

Illus. 148. Pulpit

Also cut, from ¾″ wood, a 1½″ × 3″ piece for the pulpit. Cut the top at an angle as shown in Illus. 148.

Glue the ½″ × 4″ pieces (the seats) to the backs of the pews so that the seat is ½″ from the floor. Set these aside to dry.

While the pews dry, it is a good time to stain the inside of the church. Using a brush, next paint the pews and pulpit the desired color. The color used for the project shown here is brick red.

When the stain has completely dried, glue the pulpit in the front left corner, the end away from where the doors and steeple will be.

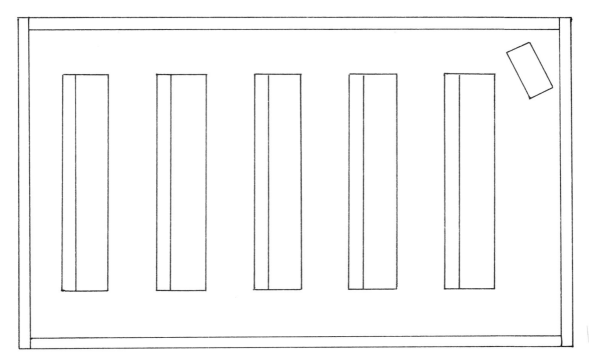

Illus. 149. Position of pews and pulpit

Then glue the pews in place, spacing them along the middle of the church (Illus. 149).

Roof

To make the roof, cut two 5½″ × 11¾″ pieces of ¼″ wood. Glue and nail these in place. Do not overlap them at the peak. To fill the gap, cut a ¼″ × ¼″ strip 11¾″ long. This will serve as the roof cap. Glue this strip in place along the roof line.

The Cross and Door Trim

Use ¼″ × ¼″ strips for the cross. Cut a 2″ piece and a 1¼″ piece. Notch out both pieces for a flush fit, and then glue them together.

From ½″ wood, cut trim pieces for around the door. Cut two strips, ¼″ × 5″, and a triangular piece to the dimensions in Illus. 150.

Glue the doors in place, carefully making sure they are right in the middle, and then glue the side trim pieces against the doors. Position the triangular trim piece over the doors, aligned with the roof peak and the mid-

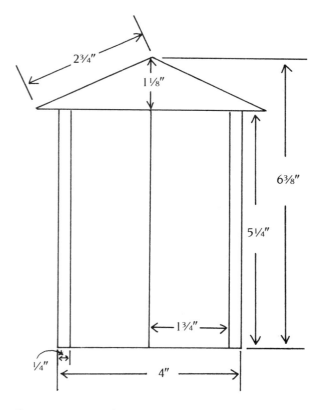

Illus. 150. Door and trim

dle of the doorway, and then glue it in place. Also glue the doorknobs in place.

Paint the cross with thalo bronze. Glue the cross above the doors, later, after the church is painted.

Also cut two ¼" × ¼" strips 5¼" long for trim below the roof edge for the end above the doors only. Glue them in place.

Steeple

From 1½" × 1½" wood, cut a base piece 1½" high. Cut out a V-shaped notch congruent with the roof angle. Then cut a 6½" piece from the 1½" × 1½" wood. Starting one inch from the bottom, taper both sides to a point, cutting away the excess with the band saw. Then sand the piece well to get a rounded effect.

Also cut a 1¾" × 2¾" piece from ¼" wood and four posts 1¾" high from ¼" × ¼" pieces.

Glue the notched base to the roof approximately two inches from the front of the roof. Glue the cap in place and then the posts (Illus. 151).

With needlenose pliers, bend a 1" brad on which to slide the bell. Then press the brad into the center bottom of the steeple (gripping the brad with the needlenose pliers). Glue the steeple in place on the posts.

Painting

A suggestion for colors used here is to paint the doors, roof, and roof cap a brick red. The trim is painted gold color. Paint the remainder of the church an ivory white.

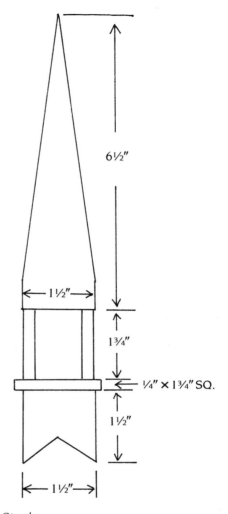

Illus. 151. Steeple

❖ **Mission Church** ❖

This flat-roofed, adobe church, reminiscent of Southwestern missions, is both delightful and easy to make (Illus. 152). Complete with bell, cross, and arched doors, this little church adds a wonderful accent when displayed with a Mexican folk art collection.

MATERIALS

Wood, ½″ thick, 8″ × 10½″
Wood, ¼″ thick, 8″ × 5½′
Wood, ¼″ × ¼″, 6″
Wood dowel, ⅜″ diameter, 12″

Illus. 152. Mission Church

Wood glue
Brass bell, ¾″ high
Brads, ¾″, No. 18, one box
Wood button plugs, ⅜″, two (doorknobs)
Coarse sand
Acrylic paint: light brick color, white

TOOLS

Table, radial-arm, or band saw
Tabletop scroll saw
Drill with ½″ bit

Tack hammer
Needlenose pliers
Small paint trowel or butter knife

INSTRUCTIONS

Basic Cutting

Using the dimensions given in Illus. 153, cut the front of the Mission Church from the ½″-thick wood. Use either a scroll saw or a band saw to cut out the step design.

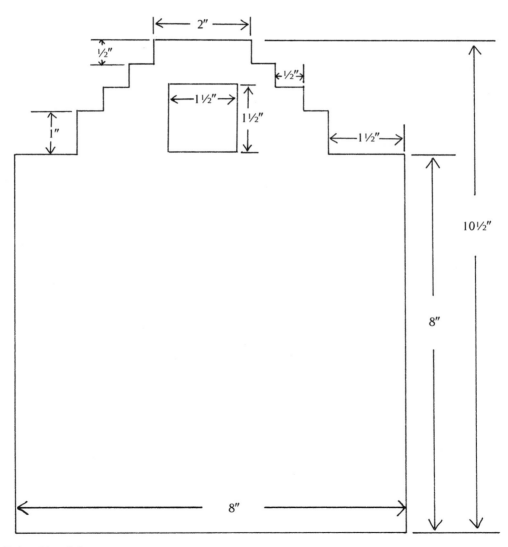

Illus. 153. Mission Church front

From the ¼" wood, cut the back (Illus. 154), the two sides (Illus. 155), and the two doors (Illus. 156).

Windows and Bell Tower

Draw the windows and the bell tower opening on the pieces according to the dimensions given in Illus. 153, and Illus. 155. Then drill a ½" hole into the middle of the area for each window and the bell tower.

Detach the blade of the scroll saw, and insert the blade through one of the holes. Reattach the blade, and cut out the area for the window opening. Repeat this procedure for the remaining windows and the bell tower.

Main Structure

Glue and nail the sides to the back. Then attach the front to the sides, measuring to keep the sides parallel and the corners square since the front extends beyond both sides (Illus. 157). Glue and nail the front to the sides.

Set the church on the remaining ¼" wood (leaving enough room to later cut out the top), and, with a pencil, trace the inside perimeter of the walls. Keep the saw blade to the outside of the pencil line to cut this piece out. Then glue and nail the floor into place.

Cut a piece for the top from the left over ¼" wood following the outside perimeter measurements of the wall. The top will rest on the sides and back and will be flush with the front wall. The dimensions are approximately 7¼" × 11½", but measure the actual construction first for an accurate fit. Glue and nail the roof in place.

Side Beams

From the ⅜" diameter dowel, cut ten 1" lengths. Glue these to the sides, approximately one inch down from the top of the

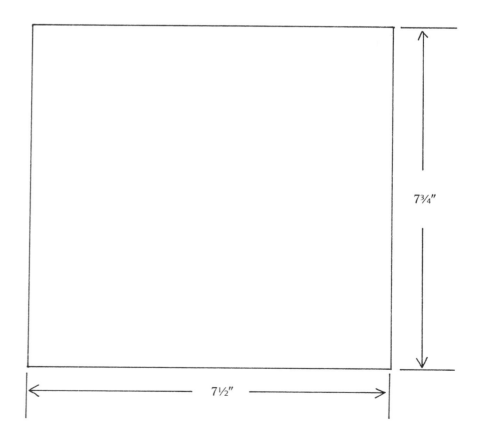

7¾"

7½"

Illus. 154. Back

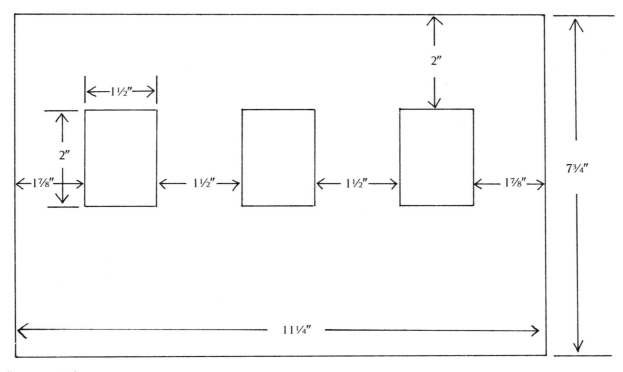

Illus. 155. Side

sides and spaced about 1⅜″ apart. Glue the middle beam first, and then measure outward.

Doors, Bell, and Cross

Cut a ¼″ × ¼″ strip of wood, and then cut it into a 2¼″ length and a 1⅜″ length. Using the band saw or scroll saw, cut a notch from both

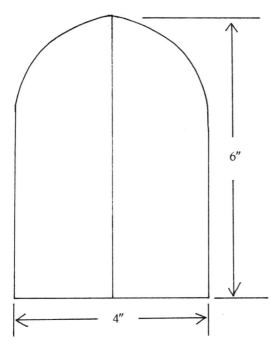

Illus. 156. Door

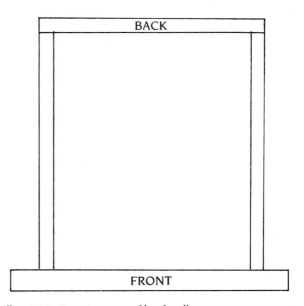

Illus. 157. Top view, assembly of walls

pieces so that they fit flush together to form the cross. Glue the pieces together.

Glue on the two doorknobs, and then paint the doors a coral-brick color along with the cross and beams. Let dry, and then glue the doors and cross in place.

Attach the bell by first bending a 1″ brad, as shown in Illus. 158. Slip the bell on the brad, and then, using needlenose pliers, push the brad into the top of the bell tower as far as it will go.

Illus. 159. Apply paint/sand mixture with a flat paint trowel or old butter knife.

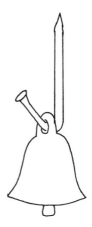

Illus. 158. Bend the brad and slide on the bell.

Adobe Finish

Mix a small amount of brick-colored paint with white paint to make a light clay color (¼ brick-colored paint with ¾ white paint). Then mix in coarse sand, using ¼ sand to ¾ paint. Mix thoroughly.

Starting at the top, apply a thin layer, using a paint trowel or old butter knife. Then continue applying the mixture to the walls of the Mission Church (Illus. 159). Be careful *not* to spread it on the doors, beams, or the cross.

Only a thin layer is necessary; however, press and spread the mixture with a firm stroke to ensure adhesion. Work carefully around the bell tower and the window edges. Use a brush as needed.

Block Buildings and Houses

❖ Block Buildings (6″–9″ High) ❖

These little buildings are simple to make (Illus. 160). The distinguishing feature is the painting that creates a special character for

Wood dowel, ¼″ diameter, 6″ length
Wood dowel, ⅛″ diameter, 8″ length
Wood, ¼″ thick, 6″ × 14″

Illus. 160. Block Buildings

each building, which is completed as you wish with details for windows, doors, and signs as well as bushes or stone work.

Luan plywood, ⅛″ thick, 6″ × 12″
Wood glue
Brads, ¾″, No. 18, one box
Sandpaper
Acrylic paint: assorted colors

MATERIALS

Wood, four-by-four (the name, not the actual dimensions): 14″ length
Wood, two-by-ten (the name, not the actual dimensions): 2′ length
Wood scrap, ¾″ thick (chimneys)

TOOLS

Band saw
Tack hammer
Paint brushes
Permanent marker: black fine-tip

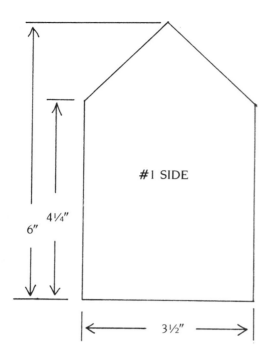

Illus. 161. #1 dimensions

Illus. 162. #1 details

INSTRUCTIONS

Basic Cutting

For this particular grouping of buildings, cut buildings #1 and #2 from the piece of four-by-four wood, according to the dimensions in Illus. 161 and 162, and Illus. 163 and 164, respectively. Use the two-by-ten length for buildings #3, #4, and #5, following the dimensions in Illus 165, Illus. 166, and Illus. 167, respectively.

From ⅛" luan plywood, cut two 2½" × 4" pieces to make a roof for building #1. Cut four triangles for building #2 to the dimensions given in Illus. 168.

Use the ¼" wood to make the roof for building #5. Cut one piece 4" × 6", and another 4" × 6¼". When the roof is attached, the longer piece will overlap at the peak.

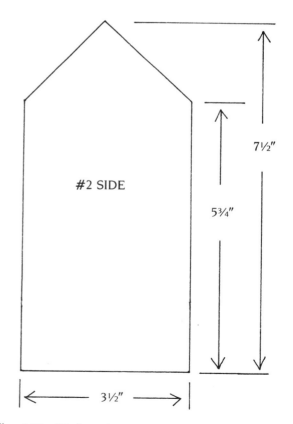

Illus. 163. #2 dimensions

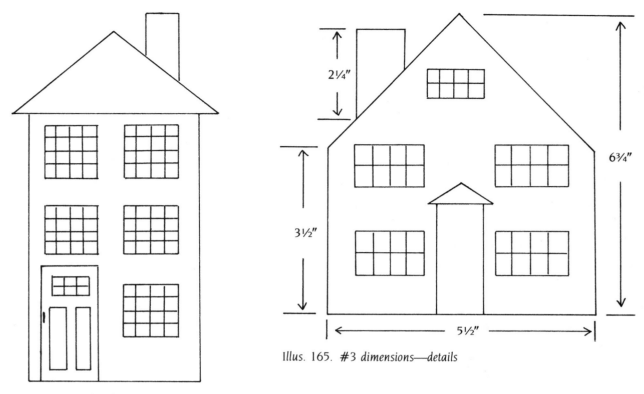

Illus. 164. #2 details

2¼"

3½"

6¾"

5½"

Illus. 165. #3 dimensions—details

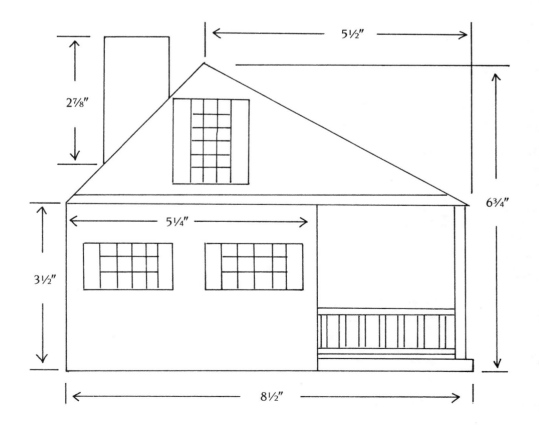

Illus. 166. #4
dimensions
—details

2⅞"

5½"

6¾"

5¼"

3½"

8½"

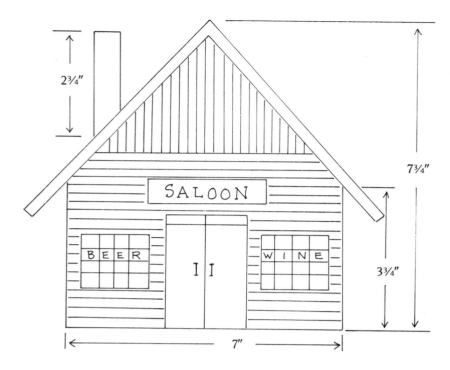

Illus. 167. #5 dimensions—details

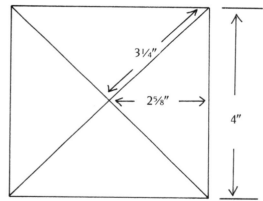

Illus. 168. #2 roof dimensions, top view

Roof, Chimney, and Trim

Glue and nail the roofs to buildings #1, #2, and #5. Sand the roof edges well, especially for building #2.

Cut chimneys from scraps of wood ranging from 1¼″ high (building #1) to 3″ high (building #5). Then for building #4, cut two 3″ pieces of ¼″-diameter dowel. Glue these in place as porch posts.

From ¼″ wood, cut two ⅛″ × 3″ pieces. Using a ⅛″ bit, drill six holes, equidistant, into these 3″ railings. Then cut six 1¼″ pieces of ⅛″ diameter dowel, and glue these into the top and bottom railings. When this assembly is dry, glue the railing into place.

Cut a thin strip from ¼″ wood, ¹⁄₁₆″ × 8½″, to use as trim across the front of building #4. Glue and nail this strip in place.

Painting

You can paint the block buildings the following suggested colors:

Building #1 — Light grey, black roof, red chimney, red and black trim

Building #2 — Dark green, gold roof, red chimney, red and gold trim

Building #3 — Gold, black roof, red chimney and door, cream windows

Building #4 — Dark grey, red roof, speckled chimney (resembling stone), red and white trim

Building #5 — Tan, tan roof, red chimney, black and white trim

Draw details (window panes, doors, etc.) with a black, permanent, fine soft-tipped marker.

❖ Tiny Block Village (1″–2″ High) ❖

This village is tiny enough that it looks great displayed above a door frame (Illus. 169). Tiny buildings and houses can be made from scraps of wood of any size. These range in size from 1⅛″ to 2″ in height and ¾″ to 1½″ wide.

MATERIALS

Wood scraps, ¾″ to 1″ thick
Wood scrap, ¼″ thick (tree cutout)
Sandpaper
Acrylic paint: assorted colors

TOOLS

Band saw
Paint brush
Permanent marker: black fine-tip (optional)

INSTRUCTIONS

Cutting

Cut small rectangles of wood, of various sizes, from the scraps of wood.

Also cut trees from the ¼″ wood scraps (Illus. 170) and bases for the trees.

Then draw the desired roof slope on the side of each rectangle. Some can be steep, some slight. The church roof, in particular, should be long and steep. Cut away the excess.

Painting

Paint these tiny houses in assorted colors; paint the roofs with contrasting colors.

Illus. 169. Tiny Block Village

Make windows using a very fine paint brush, just touching the tip to the house. If you prefer, you can use a fine-tip permanent marker to draw the windows. Also paint a small door for each tiny building.

Illus. 170. Tiny buildings—tree

Open-Front House

❖ Unfurnished House ❖

This little open house can be furnished simply or elaborately (Illus. 171). It is sturdy and can withstand many hours of play.

MATERIALS

Wood, ½" thick, 8" × 9'
Plywood, ¼" thick, 16" × 24"
Wood, ¾" thick, 8" × 24"

Wood, two-by-four, 2¼" length (optional chimney)
Wood, ¼" thick, 4" × 12"
Wood glue
Printed paper, 8 square feet (dollhouse wallpaper or small print wrapping paper)
Brick sheeting, 7½" × 11" (dollhouse brick or substitute a linoleum sample)
Rubber cement

Illus. 171. Unfurnished open-front house

Brads, 1″, No. 18, one box
Acrylic paint: medium blue, dark red (suggested)
Stain, medium color

TOOLS

Radial-arm or table saw
Band saw
Tack hammer

INSTRUCTIONS

Basic Cutting

From ½″ wood, cut: two sides, 7½″ × 9″; one floor, 7½″ × 23″; one attic floor, 7½″ × 23″; one wall, 7½″ × 8″; and two roof sections, 8″ × 14½″.

Also cut a back from ¼″ plywood according to the dimensions given in Illus. 172.

Assembly

Glue and nail the sides to the floor and to the attic floor sections (Illus. 173). Then glue and nail the center wall in place, making it equidistant from both outside walls.

Attach the plywood back at this time, also using glue and nails. Join the roof sections to the house after first sanding or angle-cutting the roof section edges so that they will join in a tight fit. The roof sections will overhang the front by about ½″ (Illus. 174). Glue the peaks together, while also gluing and fitting the sections to the back. Lay the house on its back until the roof pieces are dry. Then nail the roof pieces from the back.

An option you may want to include is a chimney cut from the two-by-four wood to measure 1″ × 1½″ × 2¼″. Cut this piece to fit the roof slope. Glue the chimney into place.

Next, cut four pieces of ½″ wood, ⅜″ × 8⅞″, to be used as corner trim. Glue this trim to the side corners, flush with the front and back.

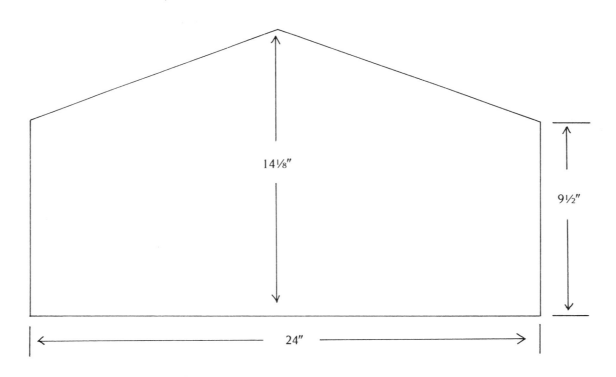

14⅛″

9½″

24″

Illus. 172. Back, ¼″ plywood

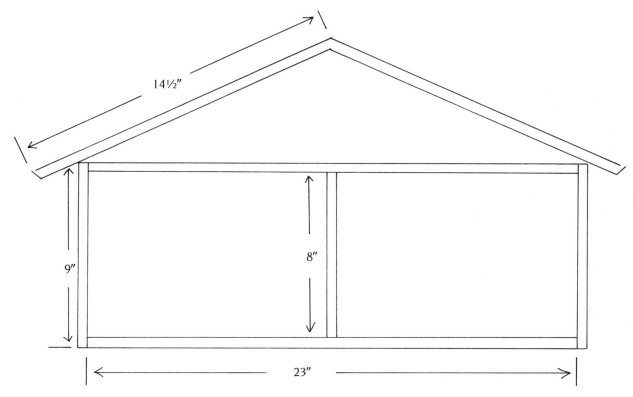

Illus. 173. Front view of house

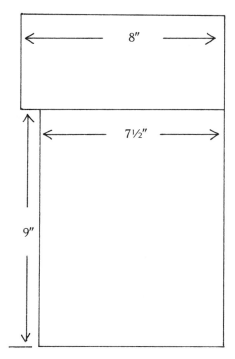

Illus. 174. Side view

Shingles

From ¾" wood, cut fifteen ¹⁄₁₆" × 24" strips. Then cut these strips into 1" pieces to be used as shingles for the roof.

Starting from the bottom, glue a row of shingles in place, extending over the lower edge about ⅛". Glue the next row in place, overlapping the first row by ⅛". Stagger each row of shingles as you work upwards.

When both sides are finished, cut a roof cap from ½" wood measuring ¼" × 8½". Glue this piece across the roof peak.

Siding

To make the siding, cut ten ⅛"-thick strips from the ¾" wood, 24" long. Cut these again into twenty-eight (28) 6½" strips, measuring first to verify the exact size needed.

Working on one side at a time, glue the first piece of siding flush with the bottom between

the corner trim. Overlapping the first piece by
⅛", glue the next piece in place, and work your
way upwards in this manner.

Floors

To begin putting the finishing touches on this
open-front house, you can follow the suggestions of staining the attic floor and the floor of
the room on the left. To add variety you can
put a brick or linoleum floor down in the other
room.

Wallpaper and Trim

Cut variously patterned paper to fit all of the
inside walls. Then attach the pieces using rubber cement since it will not buckle the paper.

An optional touch that really adds a feeling
of finished detail is to add inside trim. From
¼" wood, cut twelve ¹⁄₁₆" × 12" strips. Cut
these, to fit, for ceiling trim and baseboard
trim. Paint the trim and set it aside to dry
before gluing it into place. Use a paint color to
set off the trim from your choice of wallpaper.

Painting

One suggestion, used here, is to paint all of
the outside walls and edges a medium blue
color. The chimney is best painted a dark red
to give the impression of brick. As with all of
the projects, you may be as creative as you
would like with the choice of colors and dec-
orations, as well as with the details you choose
to include or add and options you decide to
take.

METRIC EQUIVALENCY CHART

MM—MILLIMETRES   CM—CENTIMETRES

INCHES TO MILLIMETRES AND CENTIMETRES

INCHES	MM	CM	INCHES	CM	INCHES	CM
⅛	3	0.3	9	22.9	30	76.2
¼	6	0.6	10	25.4	31	78.7
⅜	10	1.0	11	27.9	32	81.3
½	13	1.3	12	30.5	33	83.8
⅝	16	1.6	13	33.0	34	86.4
¾	19	1.9	14	35.6	35	88.9
⅞	22	2.2	15	38.1	36	91.4
1	25	2.5	16	40.6	37	94.0
1¼	32	3.2	17	43.2	38	96.5
1½	38	3.8	18	45.7	39	99.1
1¾	44	4.4	19	48.3	40	101.6
2	51	5.1	20	50.8	41	104.1
2½	64	6.4	21	53.3	42	106.7
3	76	7.6	22	55.9	43	109.2
3½	89	8.9	23	58.4	44	111.8
4	102	10.2	24	61.0	45	114.3
4½	114	11.4	25	63.5	46	116.8
5	127	12.7	26	66.0	47	119.4
6	152	15.2	27	68.6	48	121.9
7	178	17.8	28	71.1	49	124.5
8	203	20.3	29	73.7	50	127.0

Index

128